FAN PHENOMENA

BUFFY THE VA SLAY

EDITED BY
JENNIFER K. STULLER

Credits

First Published in the UK in 2013 by Intellect Books,
The Mill, Parnall Road, Fishponds, Bristol, BS16 3JG, UK

First Published in the USA in 2013 by Intellect Books,
The University of Chicago Press, 1427 E. 60th Street,
Chicago, IL 60637, USA

Editor: Jennifer K. Stuller

Series Editor and Art Direction: Gabriel Solomons

Design support: Chris Brown

Copy Editor: Emma Rhys

A Catalogue record for this book is available from
the British Library

Fan Phenomena Series
ISSN: 2051-4468
eISSN: 2051-4476

Fan Phenomena: Buffy The Vampire Slayer
ISBN: 978-1-78320-019-1
ePUB ISBN: 978-1-78320-096-2
ePDF ISBN: 978-1-78320-095-5

Printed and bound by
Bell & Bain Limited, Glasgow

Contents

Acknowledgements

I was late to the Buffy party. Having ignored enthusiastic praise from friends, as well as recommendations from family, it wasn't until I read Tim Goodman's review of the seminal sixth season musical episode, 'Once More With Feeling', in the *San Francisco Chronicle* that I decided to give it a chance.

In that one episode I fell in love – and recognized what I'd been missing; a funny, intelligent, emotionally resonant, creative, layered, and subversive serial that I should have been paying attention to all along.

Since that night of singing and dancing from Scoobies, demons, and residents of Sunnydale, California, I've been a fan. More than that, my fandom has been expressed in ways I'd never before considered, thus connecting me to friends and colleagues – many of whom were directly critical to the making of this book.

First I'd like to commend the contributors to this anthology for their flexibility and their creativity, as well as for their presentations of smart accessible research, and their unique, often personal, meditations on fandom.

My gratitude extends to the Buffy as Archetype: Rethinking Human Nature in the Buffyverse course co-creators and participants from Winter 2004 at the University of Washington. Along with those thinkers, and those in the Whedon Studies Association, I was able to see that both *Buffy* and scholarship have many points of entry – and that the show itself is a connective force.

I want to especially thank Dr. Amy Peloff. Like, Buffy Summers, you share the power. (Plus you are very smart, and very pretty.)

I'd mentioned my fandom for the series has been expressed in unexpected and extraordinary ways, so on that note I'd like to thank, Jessica Obrist, for helping me express my fandom for *Buffy* in a way I'd never imagined – performing as Joyce Summers in 2012's Whedonesque Burlesque. Thanks also go to the cast and crew for helping me conquer Fear Itself like a Slayer, and to my husband, Ryan Wilkerson, who responded to my request for a transportable six-foot tall, Monolith-like replica of the MILKBAR from the season three episode, 'Band Candy,' for my first-ever burlesque act with a 'Can do!' – and sat in the audience all five nights of the show run smiling and cheering for every act, every night.

A woman needs Scoobies, and I'm ever-grateful to have them in spades.

I'd like to thank photographers Jules Doyle, Inti St. Claire, and Sayed Alamy for sharing their work in this text, as well as the subjects for agreeing to use of their image. Al Lykya and Allexa Lee Laycock deserve a shout-out for recreating the epic Spike and Buffy liplock at GeekGirlCon '12's 'Once More With Feeling' sing-along. Thank you also to Clinton McClung, Seattle's own Sweet, for bring his event to the convention and for agreeing to be interviewed for this anthology.

Thank you also to Nikki Stafford, Rhonda Wilcox, and Scott Allie for their interviews. Many thanks to Aub Driver at Dark Horse for providing images from the canonical *Buffy* comics.

I'm grateful to Katrina Hill and Clare Kramer for inviting me to participate in the 2012 Comic-Con panel on 'Comics and the Whedonverse' – as well as to Travis Langley, Alex Langley, Brian Keathley, and Geek Nation for their support.

Suzanne Scott was my go-to reference source on fan studies, and I am grateful for her scholarship. I'd also like to thank the organizers of the Comics Arts Conference, the Slayage Conference on the Whedonverses, and The Whedon Studies Association for their continued support.

A special mention of Ensley Guffey is in order for thinking the Fan Phenomena series was a project I might be interested in – and for sending the call for editors my way.

Nancy Holder and Belle Holder have also offered friendship and support during this project. And I'd like to thank Jane Espenson for being an all-around awesome woman.

This book would not have happened without Fan Phenomena series editor Gabriel Solomons. I'm proud to have my name on such a beautifully designed book. So thank you for making our words look so good.

Finally, my love to Giles & Wesley, the two best four-footed Watchers a Slayer could hope for.

Introduction
Jennifer K. Stuller, Editor

→ **No one can predict what might become a cult phenomenon – something loved and quoted long after its debut, or its finale. A flop at the cinema might be a sensation on DVD, a comic-book superhero might still be a franchise icon decades after two kids in Cleveland created him, a humanistic series set in outer space might teach about acceptance, hope, and possibility – inspiring real-life accomplishments, and a cheerleader in a dark alley might forever influence the ways we think about what constitutes a hero.**

Except, that cheerleader was created to be a figure of identification and devotion. As Joss Whedon famously told the *A.V. Club* in 2001:

I designed *Buffy* to be an icon, to be an emotional experience, to be loved in a way that other shows can't be loved. [...] I wanted her to be a cultural phenomenon. I wanted there to be dolls, Barbie with kung-fu grip. I wanted people to embrace it in a way that exists beyond, 'Oh, that was a wonderful show about lawyers, let's have dinner'. I wanted people to internalize it, and make up fantasies where they were in the story, to take it home with them, for it to exist beyond the TV show. And we've done exactly that. [...] she has become an icon, and that's what I wanted. What more could anybody ask?

Buffy the Vampire Slayer first appeared in an eponymous 1992 film written by Joss Whedon. While that project didn't quite turn out how he wanted it to, once noting that upon the film's premiere he sat in the theatre crying, thinking he would never work again, he got another chance at fulfilling his vision of a feminist icon five years later in 1997 with a *Buffy the Vampire Slayer* television series. Four years after the TV series ended in 2003, it rose again, like Buffy from the grave, to continue in comic book form with a serialized, canonical narrative published by Dark Horse Comics with Whedon serving as Executive Producer.

Why, when *Buffy* bowed over ten years ago, is it still so important to fans? And what are the ways in which they express their continued devotion to, and deep relationship with, the *Buffy*verse? The chapters in *Buffy the Vampire Slayer and Fan Phenomena* provide answers to these questions, specifically exploring ways fans internalize, celebrate, critique, and are inspired by this landmark series, and hopefully, simultaneously provoking a larger conversation about the relationship between cult properties and fandom – particularly in regards to fan creation.

Fan phenomena can manifest in personal expression, including identification through cosplay, crafts and performance. Phenomena also has the power to be political or otherwise provide critical or social commentary on cultural expectations or more, as fans reappropriate and recontextualize their source material.

Fan phenomena is also critical to the formation of community – achieved through the writing and sharing of fanfiction, discussion boards, meet-ups, charity screenings, and other public events and gatherings including singalongs, fan conventions, academic conferences, nerdy burlesque performances, marathon screenings in living rooms, a great online global rewatch of the entire series, and discussion in the classroom.

Fandom for *Buffy* must also be considered in the production of entertainment media, particularly any involving a young, female, heroic protagonist. Because the series was extraordinarily groundbreaking, subsequent entertainment media must necessarily note the influence from a marketing standpoint. But, we've also seen that producers and writers of television shows featuring female action leads were fans of *Buffy* themselves

Introduction
Jennifer K. Stuller

– proving, as Nancy Holder, author of *BtVS* tie-in novels and series guides, rightly notes in *Finding Serenity* (2005), that, 'No work of popular culture is a spheroid unto itself'.

The first and last chapters, 'A Brief History of the Best, Worst, Known, and Not-So Known, Pop Culture Influences on the *Buffy*verse' by Jennifer K. Stuller and 'Unlimited Potentials', by Arthur Smith and David Bushman illustrate how pop culture influenced Whedon in his creation of *BtVS*, and how a line can be drawn from Whedon's source material, through to the entertainment narratives that are in turn inspired by *Buffy*. From *The X-Men* (Stan Lee & Jack Kirby, 1963) and *Night of the Comet* (Thom E. Eberhardt, 1984) through to Bo Dennis of *Lost Girl* (Michelle Lovretta, 2010) and Rose Tyler of *Doctor Who* (Russell T Davies, 2005-10), the thread, of course, is fandom itself.

In, '"Let's Watch A Girl": Whedon, Buffy and Fans in Action', Tanya R. Cochran discusses how Whedon utilizes his relationship with his fans, whom he affectionately refers to as 'peeps', to inspire them towards feminist action – particularly in response to the stoning murder of Du'a Khalil Aswad, and the intersections between social justice, transnational feminism, and the relevance of women's representation in popular culture.

Mary Kirby-Diaz provides a brief history of ficcing and 'shipping in fanfiction in her chapter, 'Ficcers and 'Shippers: A Love Story' as well as the unique specifics of how that phenomena plays out in the *Buffy*verse.

In '*Buffy*speak: The Internal and External Impact of Slayer Slang', Liz Medendorp looks at how the language of the *Buffy*verse has seeped into American culture. David Boarder Giles and Amy Peloff share how fandom for *Buffy* can be utilized in the classroom by both students and teachers in '"Welcome to the Hellmouth": Harnessing the Power of Fandom in the Classroom'.

Lorna Jowett's '*Buffy*, Dark Romance and Female Horror Fans' looks at how representations of romance, sexuality and gender in modern dark romance narratives, from *Twilight* (Stephenie Meyer, 2005-08) to *True Blood* (Alan Ball, 2008-), are influenced by *Buffy*. Kristen Julia Anderson shares how fanfiction writing communities serve as ways to continue the relationship of Willow and Tara in her contribution, 'Seeing Green: Willow and Tara Forever'.

Nikki Faith Fuller looks at 'The Art of *Buffy* Crafts' and how crafting can mirror the themes of the *Buffy*verse, most notably, in the creation of communities. And building on the theme of communities, Anthony R. Mills explores '*Buffy*verse Fandom as Religion'.

When we talk about fans as consumers and celebrants of popular culture, as well as producers of fan media, we'd be remiss not to mention Henry Jenkins's concept of 'Textual Poachers', detailed in his 1992 book of the same name – a reference to fans who raid mass culture, claiming its materials for their own use.

Poachers rework favoured media texts and representations as the basis for their own

Fig.1: Poachers rework favoured media texts and representations as the basis for their own cultural creations. Here, performer Solange Corbeau poses as Faith Lehane. Corbeau performed an act as Faith in 'Whedonesque Burlesque' - produced by Jo Jo Stilletto Events in Seattle, Washington. Nerd Burlesque, as known as 'Nerdlesque', allows fans to perform their fandom with new narratives - much like live-action fanfiction. Corbeau says, 'If I had to pick a character from the Whedonverse that my burlesque persona was most like, it would be this one'. (Photo Credit: Inti St. Clair, http://intistclair.com/, 2012)

cultural creations and social interactions, though Jenkins now more commonly refers to 'convergence culture' and 'participatory media' – and has observed in recent years that participatory culture is changing. Fans are no longer 'rogue readers' nor 'poachers' per se, because, as he notes in his introduction to *Fandom: Identities and Communities in a Mediated World* (2007), the discussion has moved towards 'consumers as active participants'.

Whedon, as a fan himself, invites us to 'poach' – declaring fans should bring their own subtext to the table, and saying of phenomena like fanfiction, that there isn't a better barometer of the kind of success that he craves, which is that people haven't only enjoyed the work; they've internalized it.

Jenkins claims that while the texts themselves may or may not be inherently empowering, what fans do with favoured texts has the potential to be. As the *Buffy*verse is already an empowering narrative, oft-described as 'subversive' and 'feminist', *Buffy* fans have a wealth of deeply resonant, and very human source material at the ready. They take this material a step further by creating new narratives through fanfiction, media manipulation and performance. They voice concerns, express and celebrate fandom, and create transformational communities not unlike the Scoobies themselves. ●

~~~~~~~~~~~

GO FURTHER

Books

Buffy: The Making of a Slayer
Nancy Holder
(Seattle: 47North, 2012)

Buffy Season 9
Joss Whedon, et al.
(Milwaukie, OR: Dark Horse 2011–)

The Buffyverse Catalog: A Complete Guide to 'Buffy the Vampire Slayer' and 'Angel' in Print, Film, Television, Comics, Games and Other Media, 1992-2010
Don Macnaughtan
(North Carolina: McFarland & Co, 2011)

Ink-Stained Amazons and Cinematic Warriors: Superwomen in Modern Mythology
Jennifer K. Stuller
(London: I.B. Tauris, 2010)

Introduction
Jennifer K. Stuller

Buffy Season 8
Joss Whedon, et al.
(Milwaukie, OR: Dark Horse, 2007–11)

Textual Poachers: Television Fans and Participatory Culture
Henry Jenkins
(New York: Routledge, 1992)

Enterprising Women: Television Fandom and the Creation of Popular Myth
Camile Bacon-Smith
(Philadelphia: University of Pennsylvania Press, 1992)

Extracts/Essays/Articles

'The Great Buffy Rewatch of 2011 Archive'
Nikki Stafford
Nik at Nite. 29 December 2011,
http://nikkistafford.blogspot.com/2011/03/great-buffy-rewatch-archive.html.

'The Onion A.V. Club Interview with Joss Whedon'
Tasha Robinson, Joss Whedon
In David Lavery and Cynthia Burkhead (eds.) *Joss Whedon: Conversations*
(Jackson, Mississippi: University of Mississippi Press, 2011. Pp. 23-33

'Buffy vs Edward: Twilight Remixed'
Jonathan McIntosh
Rebellious Pixels. 20 June 2009,
http://www.rebelliouspixels.com/2009/buffy-vs-edward-twilight-remixed.

'Introduction'
Henry Jenkins
In Jonathan Gray, Cornel Sandvoss, and C. Lee Harrington (eds.) *Fandom: Identities and Communities in a Mediated World* (New York: NYU Press, 2007), pp. 1-16

'I Want Your Sex'
Nancy Holder
In Jane Espenson (ed.). *Finding Serenity: Anti-heroes, Lost Shepherds And Space Hookers In Joss Whedon's Firefly* (Dallas: Smart Pop, 2005), pp. 139-153

Film and Television

Buffy the Vampire Slayer. Seasons 1–7
(Joss Whedon, The WB 1997–2001; UPN 2001-2003)

Websites

Fanlore, http://fanlore.org/

Organization for Transformative Works, http://transformativeworks.org/

Chapter
1

A Brief History of the Best, Worst, Known, and Not-So Known, Pop Culture Influences on the *Buffy*verse (Or, Joss Whedon's Fandom: 101)

Jennifer K. Stuller

→ I have a lot of influences. So many, in fact, that I can't even think of them all. I've sort of hodge-podged together my favorite bits of everything. I take what I need for the series'.
- Joss Whedon, quoted in *The Watcher's Guide Volume 1* (1998)

Marvel Comics and B-movie action heroines, westerns and The Muppets, teen drama, *The Simpsons* (Matt Groening, 1989-) and genre changing vampire films – all and more have influenced writer, director and producer, Joss Whedon. From comics to television to genre to film, 'We know,' as David Lavery wrote for the journal *Slayage* in 2002, 'quite a lot about Whedon's influences,' and Whedon himself told the *Official Buffy the Vampire Slayer Magazine* in 2004 there are 'almost too many to name'. He even revealed to *SFX Magazine* in 2012 that 'professorial shout-outs are a weakness' as well as a slew of previously unmentioned inspirations, saying, 'I've tried to come up with people you might not be aware of. I do have a few'.

But Whedon's influences are more than just a pop cultural hodgepodge reflected in his work, because Whedon is *himself* a fan – an unabashed and vocal fan, sharing with *his* fans not just his plethora of influences but his pleasure, and where inspiration and delight might intersect by letting fans share in his joy for culture, pop or otherwise.

The true key to understanding his work lies not merely in exploring his influences. Recognizing, investigating and even sharing in his fandom, provides nuance to our interpretations of his works. As Roz Kaveney observes in her 2008 book, *Superheroes! Capes and Crusaders in Comics and Film*, creatives such as Whedon have 'an obsessive habit of popular culture intertextuality in their dialogue and plotting […] and their core work tropes are often derived from the favorite reading and viewing of their youth'.

While staffers at Mutant Enemy, the production company behind *Buffy*, brought their own fandoms to the series, Buffy is Joss, and Joss is Buffy – as he acknowledged in a 2012 interview with *Forbes*, 'I didn't realize until after seven seasons of "Buffy" – literally, until after I was done with it – that I was writing about myself'.

To truly understand *Buffy the Vampire Slayer* and its impact, not just on popular culture, but on fan phenomena, we must not merely explore Whedon's influences, but make efforts to understand how his enjoyment of, and often reverence for, the source material is invested in his work, by exploring the source material itself. It is useful to have at least a working knowledge of where, as Kaveney says, Whedon's core tropes originated.

The series is filled with reference to often recognizable pop culture sources. From *The X-Files* (Chris Carter, 1993-2002) to *Star Wars* (George Lucas, 1977) – even 1970s sex symbol Burt Reynolds gets a mention. Each serve to further illustrate a point, emphasized by the viewer's familiarity with the referenced material. For example, Giles is generally the Fox Mulder-esque believer in the paranormal. When accused by Buffy of trying to 'Scully' her (Scully being Mulder's converse – the rational skeptic) audiences familiar with *The X-Files* are in on the joke. (See Chapter 'Buffyspeak' for more.) The Trio show an obssession for *Star Wars* and Bond-related minutia that parallels that of the Mutant Enemy writer's room – as Doug Petrie told the *Official Buffy the Vampire Slayer Magazine* in 2007, 'You could have put a tape recorder in the middle of the writers' room and recorded it verbatim, and you would have had the geeks dialogue. Their references were our references'. And Joyce, in full teenage mode after the consump-

A Brief History of the Best, Worst, Known, and Not-So Known,
Pop Culture Influences on the *Buffy*verse
(Or, Joss Whedon's Fandom: 101)
Jennifer K. Stuller

tion of magically dosed 'band candy' reveals that the epitome of male sexuality in her teenage dreams is Burt Reynolds.

An entire text (perhaps even encyclopedia or wiki) could be devoted to the characters referenced and narratives mined for *Buffy* – a series that Whedon once said he wanted to be '*My So-Called Life* meets *The X-Files*'. One could even write at length on speculated references. (For example, is Anya's fear of bunnies a nod to Whedon's love of *Monty Python's Flying Circus* [Graham Chapman, John Cleese, Terry Gilliam, Eric Idle, Terry Jones, Michael Palin, 1969-74] and the bunny with horrifying teeth in *Monty Python and The Holy Grail* [Terry Gilliam, Terry Jones, 1975]?)

Alas, this chapter must be restrained to a brief introduction to some of the key pop culture influences on the *Buffy*verse. While this book looks at aspects of fan phenomena and *Buffy the Vampire Slayer*, *Buffy the Vampire Slayer* is itself an act of fan phenomena in which the tropes and material that influenced Whedon were used to create a new narrative.

Blade the Vampire Slayer
Conceptualized by writer, Marv Wolfman, and illustrated by Gene Colan, Blade was a vampire hunter and one of the first black superheroes. He premiered in Marvel Comics' *Tomb of Dracula* issue #10 (1973). Half human, half vampire, his ultimate mission of vengeance was to kill Deacon Frost – the vampire that murdered his mother while she laboured in childbirth, and thus inadvertently created Blade's hybridity.

Influence on BtVS
Whedon has mentioned Blade the Vampire Slayer in the Marvel comic book, *Tomb of Dracula*, as an influence. In a 2001 interview with Westfield Comics, Whedon said of the 1970s subway flashback scene with Spike and Nikki Wood from the fifth season *BtVS* episode, 'Fool for Love' (Season 5, Episode 7) that there was 'much of the original Blade' in the sequence. (And arguably, in Season 7, there is an allusion to Blade in Robin Wood's quest to kill Spike – the vampire that killed *his* mother, as illustrated in 'Lies my Parents Told Me' [Season 7, Episode 17].)

Doug Petrie, who wrote 'Fool for Love' – as well as the *Tales of the Slayers* (2002) comic book tie-in, 'Nikki Goes Down!', with *Tomb of Dracula* artist, Gene Colan, is a self-proclaimed 'big 1970s Blaxploitation freak'. We can assume that certain heroines of the genre played into Nikki Wood's characterization and though women in Blaxploitation films were often the girlfriend of the hyper-masculine hero of the story, the genre also contributed the first films to feature black women in action hero roles, and even more revolutionarily, as lead protagonists.

Trivia
Blade was adapted into a film in 1998. According to a 2005 interview with Marv Wolf-

Fig.1: 'She's like Dark Phoenix
up there!' Willow Rosenberg's
(Alyson Hannigan) journey to
the dark side mirrors that of
Marvel Comics', Jean Grey,
in the classic Uncanny X-Men
story, 'The Dark Phoenix
Saga'
'Two to Go', Buffy the Vampire
Slayer (Doug Petrie, Bill
L Norton, 2002, Mutant
Enemy)

man in *Back Issue* magazine, neither he nor Gene Colan
was ever consulted on the Blade films, and even had to buy
their own tickets to see a screening.

Fan influence seen in episodes/issues
'Fool for Love' (Season 5, Episode 7) , 'Lies My Parents
Told Me' (Season 7, Episode 17) , 'Tales of the Slayers' (Dark
Horse Comics, 2002).

Dark Phoenix Saga
A pivotal and highly influential X-Men story arc during the
creative run of John Byrne and Chris Claremont (see section: 'The X-Men'), the Dark Phoenix Saga tells the tragedy
of mutant Jean Grey as she realizes her full potential, suc-
cumbs to, and is corrupted by great power – resulting in
the death of billions – before sacrificing herself to prevent
the further destruction of the solar system, and possibly
the entire universe.

Fan influence on *BtVS*
Jean Grey has been referenced in Willow Rosenberg's storyline and characterization. Or, rather more specifically,
the woman Jean Grey becomes after bonding with the abstract cosmological principle
known as Phoenix. Initially, this was a sacrifice Jean made to protect her teammates,
but the Phoenix infused her with unimaginable power. Alas, Jean could not contain such
power, it became unstable, and as with Willow, this intense amount of power corrupted
her. (Though it's still debated in nerd circles as to whether Jean was actually corrupted,
if she was possessed, or if she enjoyed the power.) Regardless, like Willow, Dark Phoenix's desires were an insatiable pursuit that made her dangerously destructive.

There are superficial similarities in the narratives and character evolutions of Jean
and Willow. They are both telepathic, have red hair, have a strong father figure (which is
actually true of most female heroes) and a dark side – one which, I would add, they both
take immense pleasure in indulging.

Fan influence seen in episodes
The Dark Willow storyline mirrors the the Dark Phoenix Saga both visually and narratively, and is specifically referenced by Andrew in the Season 6 episode 'Two to Go' (Episode
21) when he says, 'She's like Dark Phoenix up there!'

A Brief History of the Best, Worst, Known, and Not-So Known,
Pop Culture Influences on the *Buffy*verse
(Or, Joss Whedon's Fandom: 101)
Jennifer K. Stuller

Kitty Pryde
Kitty was created by John Byrne, subsequently developed by Chris Claremont, and debuted in January of 1980 in *Uncanny X-Men* #129. She was an adorable young teenager that could walk through walls – her mutant power being the ability to phase through solid objects.

Influence on *BtVS*
Whedon wrote in the introduction to the trade paperback of *Fray* (Dark Horse Comics, 2003) that Kitty Pryde was 'both a source of affection and identification' for him and 'was not a small influence on Buffy'.

Kitty went through all the adolescent trials we saw on *BtVS*: fear of change – especially in the people around her (and most alarmingly for a child, in trusted authority figures), insecurities about romantic relationships, the building of deep and meaningful friendships, rebellion and frustration (again, mostly with regards to authority figures – trusted or otherwise), rites of passage and the unique challenges associated with her gift. As with the Scoobies, readers got to watch Kitty grow up – some even grew up with her.

We know Kitty remains important to Whedon, as he agreed to write *The Astonishing X-Men* title only if he could use her character. (See the concluding chapter, 'Unlimited Potentials' for more.)

Fig.2: Xander enthusiastically explains Kitty Pryde's powers to an unamused Buffy
Buffy the Vampire Slayer
Season 8 Issue #32 (Brad Meltzer, Georges Jeanty,
© 2010, Dark Horse Comics)

Trivia
While Kitty Pryde may be 'the mother of Buffy', as Whedon told *Wired* in 2012, she is also reflected in Willow Rosenberg, a character who shares with Kitty Pryde a talent for computer skills, as well as Jewish faith.

Influence seen in episodes/issues
Seen throughout the series, and notably in a playful nod in issue #32 of Dark Horse Comics' *Buffy the Vampire Slayer Season 8* (2010). While testing out her new enhanced superpowers, Xander asks Buffy if she can 'phase'. Explaining that that means

'You can control your molecules ... and mess up machinery ... and - - and - - and - - and you're really cute, and you have this spunky personality and you're not afraid of the tough guys who everyone else is terrified of'. (Humorously, Buffy doesn't see the appeal.)

Fig.3: The Lost Boys, David (Kiefer Sutherland) and Spike (James Marsters) 'Vamp Out' The Lost Boys (© 1987, Warner Brothers) 'The Harsh Light of Day' Buffy the Vampire Slayer (Jane Espenson, James A Conter, © 1999, Mutant Enemy)

The Lost Boys

In *The Lost Boys* (Joel Schumacher, 1987), a recently divorced woman and her two sons move to the fictional beach town of Santa Carla, California to live with the family patriarch. Plagued by missing persons and gang activity, Santa Carla is the so-called 'murder capital of the world'. The truth, of course, just as it is in the fictional town of Sunnydale, is that the town is infested with vampires.

Director Joel Schumacher changed the original script from a story about young kids fighting vampires (presumably grade-school aged children as in *The Monster Squad* – also from 1987, [Director, Fred Dekker]) to a sexy movie about teenage vamps, making *Lost Boys* what he calls his '*Goonies* go vampire' – referencing the adventure film about misfits seeking pirate treasure. But Schumacher's adventure was infused with 'exotic' gypsies and 'bad-boy' motorcycles.

Lost Boys, was, as he noted, a film liberally peppered with irresistible, if dangerous, young men – men who were terribly sexy monsters. Reflecting on the appeal of vampires over other traditional monsters (like those from Universal Horror films of the mid-twentieth century that influenced Mutant Enemy writer, David Fury), Schumacher declared in the 2004 documentary featurette, 'Fresh Blood: A New Look at Vampires', that: 'The werewolf is not sexy. Frankenstein is not sexy. The Mummy is not sexy'. He claims, 'Vampires are the most fun monsters to do because they're very, very, very, sexy'.

Fan influence on *BtVS*

As we know from Whedon, who originally didn't want sexy vamps, they are in fact *so* sexy, that even lack of blood flow doesn't preclude the ability to 'get it up'. As he told Jeff Jenson of *Entertainment Weekly* in 2002, even though they are The Undead, 'If vampires couldn't have erections, our show would have been 12 episodes long'.

So besides the elements of comedy, horror and family drama, pop culture and literary references, and The Sexy, what else of *Lost Boys* can we see in *Buffy the Vampire Slayer*? Or, where is the line from the 'Blood-Sucking Brady Bunch' to the 'Scooby Gang?'

We know from Whedon himself that the idea 'Vamping Out' came from *Lost Boys*, and that the vampire Spike has a little of Kiefer Sutherland's character, David, in him. Other similarities to *Buffy the Vampire Slayer* include: a fictional Southern California town (Santa Carla and Sunnydale), vamps living in a residence sunken by an earthquake, rock star look-a-likes (Jim Morrison via Jason Patric's Michael, and Billy Idol via James

A Brief History of the Best, Worst, Known, and Not-So Known,
Pop Culture Influences on the *Buffy*verse
(Or, Joss Whedon's Fandom: 101)
Jennifer K. Stuller

Marsters's Spike, respectively) and *hoyay!* (an internet fandom term, aka: 'homoeroticism – Yay!').

Seen in episodes
'Bumpy' faces, bumping naughty-bits and swanky cave-dwelling seen throughout the series run.

Muppets
The Muppets were a group of lovable, misfit characters, brought together by their oft-frazzled, but always supportive, leader Kermit the Frog. Kermit, created in 1955, appeared on *Sesame Street* (Joan Ganz Cooney and Lloyd Morrisett,1969-), in *Muppet* movies and *The Muppet Show* (Jim Henson, 1976-81), a television series that aired from 1976–81. The show featured Kermit as the stage manager of a vaudeville show filled with wacky performers.

Fig.4: Rachel Jackson, owner of Vox Fabuli Puppets in Seattle Washington, poses with her creation 'Puppet Joss' - a tribute to the convergence of puppet fandom and the Whedonverse for the production 'Whedonesque Burlesque' (Photo Credit: Inti St. Clair, http://intistclair.com/, 2012)

Fan influence on *BtVS*
Jim Henson was a puppeteer, voice actor and Kermit the Frog's alter ego. As Head Archivist for the Jim Henson Company, Karen Falk, has said, he was 'a gatherer of talent'. And just as Henson *is* The Muppets, specifically Muppet Kermit the Frog, Joss Whedon *is Buffy the Vampire Slayer*, specifically, Buffy Summers.

Whedon's father, Tom Whedon, worked for the Children's Television Workshop – the company responsible for creating the edutainment programs *Sesame Street* and *The Electric Company* (1971-77). As detailed in Michael Davis's 2008 *Street Gang: The Complete History of Sesame Street*, the creators of *Sesame Street* regularly drank together after-hours. Sometimes this was at a bar, but often it was at the elder Whedon's apartment. Artists, writers, musicians and actors gathered to there to imbibe, and thus young Joss grew up surrounded, and no doubt formed, by lively creatives.

Fan influence on *BtVS*
Joss Whedon claimed in a featurette for the 2004 DVD set of the fifth season of *Angel* that the episode, 'Smile Time', is a shout-out to his father. Whedon confirms puppets were a big thing in his life when he was a kid, and notes in an issue of the *Official Angel Fan Magazine* that: 'A lot of our friends and family were Muppet people. We were part of a whole Muppety circle'. (2004)

And while Whedon has not mentioned Henson himself as a direct inspiration, but rather the Muppety people, it could be argued that Whedon is a spiritual creative successor to Henson. Both have created entertainment with a message, utilized old media in new ways, experimented with new ways of storytelling, and are great gatherers of talent.

Influence seen
Throughout the series – particularly in Buffy's leadership skills, her gathering of misfits to create a family, and her loving support of their varied talents.

Near Dark
Near Dark, also from 1987, was directed by Kathryn Bigelow, and co-written by her and Eric Red. The film, which was overshadowed by *Lost Boys*, is the story of Caleb, a young man in Oklahoma, who encounters the mysterious, Mae, one night. After a make-out session that ends with a life-altering bite, Caleb begins an uncomfortable physical transformation and is kidnapped by Mae's rag-tag family. This clan of vicious transients intends to kill Caleb, but Mae, smitten with the handsome cowboy, manages to have his life temporarily saved.

Part teenage love story, part road movie and part western, *Near Dark* is strange and haunting. Richard Corliss of *Time* called the film the 'all-time teenage vampire love story' – though, the word vampire itself is never used once throughout the film. Then again, it could be argued that *Near Dark* isn't really a film *about* vampires. As Stacey Abbott notes in her 2007 book, *Celluloid Vampires*, in *Near Dark* (as well as *The Lost Boys*) the vampire serves as an allegory for the bodily changes of adolescence. And as Whedon said of *Buffy* in a 2010 issue of *Entertainment Weekly*, 'Ultimately, my show was less about vampires than most shows with *vampire* in the title'.

Influence on *BtVS*
Whedon gives nod to Kathryn Bigelow's vampire-western, *Near Dark*, 'because' as he says in *The Watcher's Guide Volume 1* (1998), 'it's so important'.

Narrative themes from *Near Dark* that parallel *Buffy the Vampire Slayer* include adolescence, rebellion and chosen family. There are also obvious visual references: Spike blacks out the windows of his vehicles in order to travel in daylight – just like Mae's family. One can suspect in a 'verse laden with observant pop culture nods that someone like Spike might have even gotten the idea from viewing the film. Additionally, he mirrors the clan patron's use of protective goggles, and a drab wool blanket to shield himself from sunlight.

Seen in episodes
'Lover's Walk' (Season 3, Episode 8), 'Pangs' (Season 4, Episode 8), 'Spiral' (Season 5, Episode 20)

Trivia
In June of 1990, a young Adrian Pasdar was named 'One to Watch' by *Sassy Magazine*.

A Brief History of the Best, Worst, Known, and Not-So Known,
Pop Culture Influences on the *Buffy*verse
(Or, Joss Whedon's Fandom: 101)
Jennifer K. Stuller

Pasdar would go on to star in the television series, *Heroes* (Tim Kring, 2006-10), which, similarly to *Buffy*, was a rewriting of the hero myth, and one that featured a cheerleader who was more than she seemed.

Night of the Comet
In this B-movie classic from 1984 (Director, Thom E. Eberhardt) – a genre mash-up of horror, sci-fi and comedy, about two teenage sisters who kick zombie ass in a post-apocalyptic So. Cal – our girl heroes are Sam and Reggie Belmont, two of the only survivors left after the Earth passes through the tail of a comet. (It could happen!)

While this natural disaster has left most everyone else on the planet turned to either red dust or zombies, the Belmont sisters survive through the magic of B-movie science and a combination of the military combat training they'd received from their father, natural quick wit and a couple of attractive allies.

Older sister, Reggie, played by Catherine Mary Stewart, recognizes the severity of the situation and stresses to her kid sister that the 'burden of civilization is upon us' – a sentiment echoed in the Slayer's burden of being the 'one girl in all the world'. Sam, played by Kelli Maroney, feels a more personal angst. In perhaps what is a response only a teenager could have to such an impossible event, she grieves not for the end of humanity, but for the fact that the boy she wanted to date is now dust. Reggie and Sam are nevertheless fearless in the face of the apocalypse, handling machine guns with the same light-heartedness and humour they'd take to the mall.

Fan influence on BtVS
Several themes from *Comet* can be detected in *Buffy*: the weapon-wielding high school cheerleader, teen angst over parents, teen angst over dead boyfriends, the blending of horror and humor, unapologetic, even celebratory, meta-level B-movie roots, and the girl that kicks monster ass – in an alley no less. The influence of *Comet* on *Buffy* is also evident in its dialogue; silly, and yet spoken by strong, smart females who wield their snarky words as well as their weapons. Lines such as 'Come here your ass,' and 'The Mac10 submachine gun was practically designed for housewives,' surely served as stylistic inspiration for *Buffy*speak: 'Yes, date, and shop and hang out and go to school and save the world from unspeakable demons. You know, I wanna do girlie stuff,' and, 'If the apocalypse comes, beep me'.

Trivia
Joss Whedon told *Entertainment Weekly* in 2010, 'There's a whole recipe for how to make a Buffy. Take one cup Sarah Connor from the first *Terminator* movie. One cup Ripley [and] three tablespoons of the younger sister from *Night of the Comet*'.

Teen angst
Music. Being misunderstood. A need for purpose and something to believe in. First loves. Heartbreak. Parents who just don't understand. Ah, the trials, tribulations and occasional triumphs of adolescence. Whedon has famously expressed many times that he believes that high school is a horror movie and that anyone who survives it is a hero. (In a 2001 *SFX Vampire Special* he also referred to it as 'a soap opera' and 'a ridiculous comedy'.) He's referenced several teen dramas as being influential including, but not limited to: *My So-Called Life* (Winnie Holzman, 1994-5)– the story of Angela Chase, a young woman discovering her identity; *Pretty in Pink* (John Hughes, 1986) , about Andie Walsh – a girl from the wrong side of the tracks who gets the guy; and *Pump up the Volume* (Allan Moyle, 1990) – about Mark Hunter (aka 'Hard Harry'), an awkward loner who gets the girl and starts a revolution simply by discovering a way to express himself and sharing his voice.

Influence on *BtVS*
Anytime the series focused on the confusion or pain of growing up (absent parents, boyfriends who turn evil, sexual awakenings, and so on) as well as the good times (young love, friends who'll do anything for you, saving the world).

The X-Men
Born of early 1960s Atomic-Age angst by Marvel Comics' Stan Lee and Jack Kirby, the X-Men introduced the world to the idea of super-powered mutants – beings given a wide array of abilities due to seemingly random genetic mutations, and representing a possible next step in human evolution. Helmed by various creative teams over the decades, the X-Men and its transmedia spin-offs have carried on the Marvel tradition of exploring not only the larger-than-life adventure aspects of storytelling, but also the more personal and emotional trials and triumphs of its cast of characters. Playing on central themes of societal otherness, created family, and indeed the seemingly alien transformation of the adolescent body (when mutant powers often manifest), the X-Mythos plays out across an unsympathetic world of ignorance, fear and mutant (civil) rights inequality, where our heroes are constantly challenged to remain true to their calling while at the same time, just wanting to be normal and 'fit in' with the crowd.

Influence on *BtVS*
Whedon grew up reading Marvel Comics, and has said that the X-Men are one of the biggest influences on his work there is. Where the comic would excel, and indeed flourish under the seminal run of Chris Claremont and John Byrne in the 1970s and 1980s, was in the character-driven plot lines featuring the X-Men (and its subsequent spinoff *The New Mutants* [Chris Claremont and Bon McLeod; first appearance, 1982]) as a young team led by its paterfamilias, Professor X, that grows into maturity and identity while both studying for a physics exam and saving the world (a lot). Just as the heroic X-Men

A Brief History of the Best, Worst, Known, and Not-So Known,
Pop Culture Influences on the *Buffy*verse
(Or, Joss Whedon's Fandom: 101)
Jennifer K. Stuller

are outcasts chosen by fate and bound by duty to protect the unknowing populace that fears and mistrusts them, we can see a young Buffy Summers struggling to accept her calling and gift, while endlessly performing the thankless task of saving the students of Sunnydale High – the very same people that ostracize her for being 'weird', and 'uncool'.

Additionally, the joining together of t he young misfit Scoobies under a strong father figure, and into a found family, echoes the themes of the whole being much more than merely the sum of its parts. As Roz Kaveney notes of the young X-Men in her 2008 book, *Superheroes!*,

[T]heir complex interactions, crushes on each other, desire to have relationships with missing or rejecting parents [...] their need to study, [and] to save the world, makes the Claremont period X-Men [...] at least as relevant a model for Whedon's Scoobies [...] as the original Scooby-Doo team.

Seen in episodes/issues
Throughout the series run, truly it's at the very core of the Scoobies.

Trivia
Buffy the Vampire Slayer Season 8 #35's (2010) 'Twilight' cover pays homage to Marvel Comics' *Uncanny X-Men #138* (1980) by John Byrne.

Whedon served as a script doctor for the *X-Men* movie that came out in 2000 (Director, Bryan Singer). Save a couple of lines, his work was nearly thrown out in its entirety. Only one was left the way he wrote it, and presented how he intended. The other was famously misdelivered.

Conclusion
When we talk about fan phenomena and *Buffy the Vampire Slayer*, Joss Whedon's own fandom matters because he shares his influences as a fan, allowing fans of *Buffy* a potentially more complex relationship to, and greater understanding of, the text. Thus, looking at the narratives that influenced him becomes critical to an understanding of how Whedon utilizes pop culture to create connective and resonant stories that provide inspiration in turn. This understanding is, of course, further enhanced by the fact that Whedon wants to share these pop culture pleasures, and sometimes, obsessions. As he wrote in the foreword to *Comic-Con Episode IV: A Fan's Hope* (2011), '[Y]ou only really connect with a fan, not just by being around them, but by being one yourself. I've never been anything but'. ●

GO FURTHER

Books

Joss Whedon: The Complete Companion – The TV Series, The Movies, The Comic Books and More
Ed. Mary Alice Money
(London: Titan Books, 2012)

The Buffyverse Catalog: A Complete Guide to 'Buffy the Vampire Slayer' and 'Angel' in Print, Film, Television, Comics, Games and Other Media, 1992–2010
Don Macnaughtan
(North Carolina: McFarland & Co, 2011)

Joss Whedon: Conversations
Eds Cynthia Burkhead and David Lavery
(Jackson, MS: University Press of Mississippi, 2011)

Buffy Season 9
Joss Whedon, et al.
(Milwaukie, OR: Dark Horse 2011–)

Buffy Season 8
Joss Whedon, et al.
(Milwaukie, OR: Dark Horse, 2007–11)

Ink-Stained Amazons and Cinematic Warriors: Superwomen in Modern Mythology
Jennifer K. Stuller
(London: I.B. Tauris, 2010)

Street Gang: The Complete History of Sesame Street
Michael Davis
(New York: Penguin Books, 2008)

Superheroes! Capes and Crusaders in Comics and Film
Roz Kaveney
(London and New York: I.B. Tauris, 2008)

A Brief History of the Best, Worst, Known, and Not-So Known,
Pop Culture Influences on the *Buffy*verse
(Or, Joss Whedon's Fandom: 101)
Jennifer K. Stuller

Celluloid Vampires
Stacey Abbott
(Austin, TX: University of Texas Press, 2007)

The Cinema of Kathryn Bigelow: Hollywood Transgressor
Deborah Jermyn and Sean Redmond Eds.
(London: Wallflower Press, 2003)

Writing Science Fiction and Fantasy Television
Joe Nazzaro
(London: Titan Books, 2002)

Tales of the Slayers
Joss Whedon et al
(Milwaukie, OR: Dark Horse, 2002)

The Watcher's Guide Vol. 1
Christopher Golden and Nancy Holder
(New York: Pocket Books, 1998)

Our Vampires Ourselves
Nina Auerbach
(Chicago: The University of Chicago Press, 1995)

The Uncanny X-Men: 'The Dark Phoenix Saga' TPB
Terry Austin, John Byrne and Chris Claremont
(New York: Marvel Comics, 1991)

Extracts/Essays/Articles

'"Avengers" Director Joss Whedon on Trying to Be More Like Buffy'
Jeff Bercovici and Joss Whedon
In *Forbes*. 3 May 2012, http://www.forbes.com/sites/jeffbercovici/2012/05/03/
avengers-director-joss-whedon-on-trying-to-be-more-like-buffy/

'Joss Whedon on Comic Books, Abusing Language and the Joys of Genre'
Adam Rogers and Joss Whedon
In *Wired*. 3 May 2012, http://www.wired.com/underwire/2012/05/joss-whedon/

'Heroes and Inspirations: Joss Whedon'
Jim McLauchlin and Joss Whedon
In *SFX*. April 2012, pp. 72–75.

'Foreword'
Joss Whedon
In Morgan Spurlock. *Comic-Con Episode IV: A Fan's Hope*
(New York: DK Publishing, 2011)

'The Ink-Stained Amazon Presents: A Brief History of the Best, Worst, Known, and
Not-So Known, Pop Culture Influences on the *Buffy*verse, Mostly'
Presented at the *Fourth Biennial Slayage Conference on the Whedonverses*,
Flagler College St. Augustine, FL, 3-6 June 2010.

'100 Greatest Characters: Buffy'
Joss Whedon
In *Entertainment Weekly*. Issue #1105–106. 4 June 2010, p. 44.

'The Lost Boys: Not Your Parents' Vampire Movie (Though It Might Be By Now)'
Suzette Chan
In *Sequential Tart*. 26 April 2010, http://www.sequentialtart.com/article.php?id=1686.

'The Story Behind The Lost Boys'
Josh Winning
In *Total Film*. 11 March 2010, http://www.totalfilm.com/news/the-story-behind-the-lost-boys.

'Jim Henson's Fantastic World: A Retrospective'
Jennifer K. Stuller
In *Geek Monthly*. September 2009, pp. 40-42.

'Action!'
Manohla Dargis
In the *New York Times*. 21 June 2009.

'Growing Up With Pryde'
Jason Shayer
In *Back Issue* #33 ('Teen Heroes Issue'). March 2009, pp. 39–43.

A Brief History of the Best, Worst, Known, and Not-So Known,
Pop Culture Influences on the *Buffy*verse
(Or, Joss Whedon's Fandom: 101)
Jennifer K. Stuller

'Night of the Comet: A Grrrl on Film Recommended Cult Classic'
Jennifer K. Stuller
In *Bitch Media*. 20 July 2009, http://bitchmagazine.org/post/night-of-the-comet-a-grrrl-on-film-recommended-cult-classic

'Brought to You by the Letter S'
James Panero
In the *New York Times*. 28 December 2008.

'The New Cult Canon: *Near Dark*'
Scott Tobias
In the *A.V. Club*. 5 November 2008,
http://www.avclub.com/articles/the-new-cult-canon-near-dark,2523/

'*The Hurt Locker*: A Near-Perfect War Film'
Richard Corliss
In *TIME* Magazine. 4 September 2008,
http://www.time.com/time/arts/article/0,8599,1838615,00.html

'Claremont and Byrne: The Team that Made the X-Men Uncanny'
Al Nickerson
In *Back Issue* #29 ('Mutants Issue'). July 2008, pp. 3-12.

'The Dark Redhead: Willow and her fury. Or "Are you kidding? She's like Dark Phoenix
up there"'
Jane Martin
Presented at the *Third Biennial Slayage Conference on the Whedonverses*,
Arkadelphia, Arkansas, 5-8 June 2008.

'The Buffy Handbook Part Six: Geeks, Gone, and Grave
(Writer's Season by Season Guide)'
Joe Nazzaro
In the *Official Buffy the Vampire Slayer Magazine*. December/January 2007, pp.
44-48.

'Blade and Cyborg: Marv Wolfman on his Creations'
Michael Eury
In *Back Issue* #8. February 2005, pp. 14-16.

'The Puppet Summit'
Matt Partney
In the *Official 2004 Angel Yearbook*. pp. 60–66.

'Comics in Context #42: Joss Whedon's Comics & Stories *X-Men*, *Buffy*, and more'
Peter Sanderson
In *IGN*. 18 June 2004, http://comics.ign.com/articles/595/595614p1.html.

'End of Days'
Joe Nazzaro
In the *Official Buffy the Vampire Slayer Magazine*. February 2004, pp. 38–43.

'Joss the Vampire Scripter'
Ed Gross
In *SFX Vampire Special*. 2001, pp. 35–47.

'Foreword'
Joss Whedon
In *Fray* (TPB) (Milwaukie, OR: Dark Horse, 2003).

'An Interview with Joss Whedon'
Ken P. and Joss Whedon
In *IGN*. 23 June 2003, http://movies.ign.com/articles/425/425492p1.html.

'"A Religion in Narrative": Joss Whedon and Television Creativity'
David Lavery
Ie. *Slayage: The Journal of the Whedon Studies Association* 7 (2002).

'A Blood Good Chat With "Buffy"'s Creator'
Jeff Jenson
In *Entertainment Weekly*. 14 June 2002, http://www.ew.com/ew/article/0,,260274,00.html.

'Interview: Joss Whedon'
Tasha Robinson
In the *Onion A.V. Club*. 5 September 2001,
http://www.avclub.com/articles/joss-whedon,13730/.

'Interview with Joss Whedon'
1 July 2001
http://westfieldcomics.com/wow/low/low_int_051.html

A Brief History of the Best, Worst, Known, and Not-So Known,
Pop Culture Influences on the *Buffy*verse
(Or, Joss Whedon's Fandom: 101)
Jennifer K. Stuller

'One to Watch: Adrian Pasdar'
Christina Kelly
In *Sassy*. June 1990, p. 33.

'Film: "Night of the Comet," Adventure in California'
Vincent Canby
In the *New York Times*. 16 November 1984.

'The Dark Phoenix Tapes'
In Chris Claremont, *Phoenix: The Untold Story* (New York: Marvel Comics, 1984).

'Kelli Maroney: Drive-in Icon'
Rob Freese
In *VideoScope Magazine*. http://www.videoscopemag.com/interview_kmaroney.php.

'A Night to Remember: Thom Eberhardt tells the tale of the Comet'
Charlie Mason
In *The Ultimate Night of the Comet Fan Site*. 2004
http://www.nightofthecomet.info/interviews_thom.html.

'Retro Crush Interviews The Star of Night of the Comet and Chopping Mall'
In *Retro Crush*, 200. http://www.retrocrush.com/archive2007/kelli/.

'Catherine Mary Stewart:
A Talk With The Star of The Last Starfighter and Night of The Comet'
The Moviezzz Blog. 2009. http://talkingmoviezzz.blogspot.com/2009/10/catherine-mary-stewart-talk-with-star.html.

Films and Television

'*Angel*: The Final Season' Featurette. *Angel Season 5*
(US: 20th Century Fox Home Entertainment, 2004)

'Smile Time'. *Angel Season 5* (US: 20th Century Fox Home Entertainment, 2004)

'The Lost Boys – a Retrospective'. Featurette. *The Lost Boys*
(US: Warner Home Video, 2004).

'The Lost Boys: A Director's Vision'. Featurette. *The Lost Boys*
(US: Warner Home Video, 2004)

'Fresh Blood: A New Look at Vampires'. Featurette. *The Lost Boys*
(US: Warner Home Video, 2004)

'Hey Kids! It's Smile Time'. Featurette.
(US: 20th Century Fox Home Entertainment, 2004)

Buffy the Vampire Slayer. Seasons 1–7
(Joss Whedon, The WB 1997–2001; UPN 2001-2003)
The Lost Boys, Joel Schumacher, dir. (US: Warner Bros., 1987)

Near Dark, Kathryn Bigelow, dir. (US: F/M Entertainment, 1987)

Night of the Comet. Thom Eberhardt, dir. (US: Atlantic Releasing, 1984)

Chapter
2

'Let's Watch A Girl': Whedon, Buffy and Fans in Action

Tanya R. Cochran

→ The fans of Joss Whedon's *Buffy the Vampire Slayer* are much like any other fans. They watch and rewatch seven seasons of the television series, read and reread an eighth and ninth season of the canonical comic book. They talk online, seek each other's face-to-face fellowship, and find creative outlets to express their devotion – vids, costume replicas, drawings, paintings, performances and fanfiction. Yet there is something about Whedon and his works, especially the television series *Buffy*, which moves admirers beyond those typical expressions.

That something is Whedon's own commitment to feminist activism, one he explored and shared with fans through eponymous character Buffy Summers. In turn, some *Buffy* fans have turned on-screen action into off-screen activism by living in the world in ways that honour the spirit of the series, its central characters and creator, a spirit that challenges gender roles, sexism and ultimately the status quo. This type of fan activism doesn't just save a show. It changes the world – just like Buffy and her friends.

When asked in 2001 by the *A.V. Club*'s Tasha Robinson if he was surprised by fans' fervour for *Buffy*, Whedon admitted, 'I designed *Buffy* to be an icon, to be an emotional experience, to be loved in a way that other shows can't be loved'. From Whedon's perspective, much of that fervour came from the audience's identification with the often unpleasant, sometimes harsh developmental stage of adolescence that Buffy and her classmates go through during the early seasons of the show. (Never mind that according to the Slayer mythology, Buffy is also the only girl in the entire world who '*alone* will stand against the vampires, the demons, and the forces of darkness' [emphasis added].) Becoming an adult is probably the most difficult and important thing any of us will ever do, said Whedon, so *Buffy* purposefully showed the target teen audience that everyone who makes it through those tough years is heroic, extraordinary rather than ordinary – greater than she or he appears to be. Yet *Buffy* is about more than simply surviving puberty and high school. What makes the series and its characters compelling are the poignant moments that occur in the midst of surviving: falling in love for the first time, realizing how scary and truly evil the world can be, being disappointed or abandoned by trusted loved ones, understanding that not every mistake can be fixed, and enduring serious consequences. Though rooted in the genre of fantasy, *Buffy* deeply affected and continues to affect many viewers of all ages because they recognize themselves in the lives and experiences of Buffy, the 'Chosen *One*' (emphasis added); her best friends Willow Rosenberg and Xander Harris; her mentor Giles, the 'Watcher'; her on-again-off-again boyfriend, the vampire-with-a-soul Angel; her 'frenemies' Cordelia Chase and the vampire Spike; her mother Joyce and sister Dawn; and others. The witty and weaponized teen fighters of evil quickly grow into a 'chosen family' who affectionately call themselves the Scooby Gang, or Scoobies. Like the characters of the US cartoon series *Scooby Doo* (Hanna and Barbera,1969–present), this motley group of adolescents who hail from Sunnydale, California, must learn to rely on each other not only to defeat their foes, but also to live their lives.

In a May 2012 post on the fan-run blog *Whedonesque*, Whedon expressed his thanks to his own motley group for sticking with and by him for so many years. (Because he doesn't maintain his own website, Facebook or Twitter accounts, Whedon communicates with fans several times a year via the *Whedonesque*.) The critical and financial success of Marvel's *The Avengers* (2012) opening weekend, a film he wrote and directed, prompted Whedon to publicly remind himself what really matters: his family, friends and 'peeps' – a word he chose over *fans*, one that connotes a *community* rather than a *fol-*

'Let's Watch A Girl': Whedon, Buffy and Fans in Action
Tanya R. Cochran

Fig.1: Poster Design by Adam Levermore

lowing. He went on to say, 'If you think topping a box office record compares with someone telling you your work helped them through a rough time, you're probably new here'. This statement echoes another he made regarding the second season *Buffy* episodes 'Surprise' (Season 2, Episode 13) and 'Innocence' (Season 2, Episode 14).

In May 2000, Whedon told *Fresh Air*'s David Bianculli that the idea 'the audience has been through this' was central to everything he and his creative team were doing on *Buffy*. Real people experience joy and pain, love and loss, so the characters had to experience the same: 'We always have to be about "How does the audience relate to having done this themselves?"' In 'Surprise' and 'Innocence', Buffy celebrates her 17th birthday, and she and Angel consummate their romantic relationship. A tender and passionate first sexual encounter for Buffy turns bitter and cruel the next morning. Angel, long before re-ensouled by a Gypsy spell and, thus, cursed with human guilt and remorse, has reverted to the soulless Angelus who demeans her with insults about her obvious lack of love-making expertise and flippantly punctuates their post-pillow talk with 'I'll call ya'. Embarrassed, hurt and confused, Buffy does not yet know that because Angel experienced a moment of true happiness with her, the spell has been broken, his soul released. As Whedon told Bianculli, 'That's why when we aired 'Innocence,' [...] I went on the Internet and a girl typed in, "This is unbelievable. This exact thing happened to me," and that's when I knew we were doing the show right'. In other words, 'feeling' is essential to good storytelling. In fact, *Buffy* is about just that: emotions. 'Emotional realism is the core of the show,' said Whedon. 'It's the only thing I'm really interested in'. Most of *Buffy*'s audiences – fans, critics and scholars – agree. While emotional realism may be a meaningful and satisfying end in itself, can feelings move an invested audience beyond the pleasure of the text? Can a heart-felt personal experience become a hands-on, collective political one? For Whedon and for some of *Buffy*'s fans, the answer appears to be 'yes'. 'Yes,' with a feminist inflection.

In May 2006, the non-profit women's rights organization Equality Now honoured Whedon as a feminist media producer at their gala 'On the Road to Equality: Honoring Men on the Front Lines'. A video of a portion of the event is currently posted to the organization's YouTube page. In that video, actor and advisory board member Meryl Streep provides a brief history of Equality Now as well as introduces Whedon as the award recipient. Streep explains that the non-profit was cofounded by Jessica Neuwirth, a former high school student of Whedon's mother, Lee Stearns. Though Streep only briefly explains how Whedon and Equality Now are connected, the link seems more important than has been noted. When Whedon speaks of his mother, who died in 1992 (the same year the movie *Buffy the Vampire Slayer*, directed by Fran Rubel Kuzui, was released), he credits her for inspiring him: 'A lot of [my interest in powerful female characters such as Buffy] is inherent and studied and strongly-felt feminism. [...] I like strong women. I was raised by one,' he told Shawna Ervin-Gore of *Dark Horse Comics* in June 2001. Yet Stearns inspired not only her son. As a history teacher, she also inspired lawyer and political activist Jessica Neuwirth.

Both Whedon and Neuwirth attended the school where Lee Stearns (at the time, Lee Whedon) taught. Riverdale Country School is a private, liberal arts institution located on the northwest edge of New York City. It is a member of the Ivy Preparatory School League, making it a feeder institution for the Ivy League colleges and universities Brown, Columbia, Cornell, Dartmouth, Harvard, Princeton, the University of Pennsylvania and Yale. Designed to produce leaders, Riverdale has a list of alums that includes US Senator Edward Kennedy, musician Carly Simon, National Public Radio commentator Neal Conan, restaurant critic Tim Zagat, and, coincidentally, actor Sarah Michelle Gellar who portrayed Buffy Summers. Neuwirth graduated from Riverdale and entered the undergraduate history program at Yale where she earned her BA degree. She completed her graduate law degree at Harvard. Since then, Neuwirth has worked with Amnesty International, the United Nations and the International Criminal Tribunal in response to violence against women. As both a parent and an educator, Stearns apparently had a profound effect on the young people in her life, especially her son Joss and student Jessica. It is not surprising then that Neuwirth's Equality Now would recognize Whedon for creating culturally significant characters such as Buffy at an event titled 'On the Road to Equality'.

In his acceptance speech, Whedon first compliments the audience for their courage – for supporting Equality Now and the work it does to end violence against women. Then he launches into a role-playing performance in which he assumes dual parts: himself and an imaginary stream of reporters. He says, 'The most courageous thing I've ever done is something called a press junket, which is actually pretty courageous, believe me, because they ask you the same questions over and over and over and over and over and over'. He organizes the rest of his speech around one of those questions: 'Why do you write these strong women characters?' – Buffy being the first and, arguably, most influential. Initially, the question seems innocent enough, and his answers are sincere, thoughtful:

I think it's because of my mother. She really was an extraordinary, inspirational, tough, cool, sexy, funny woman [...]. My father and my stepfather had a lot to do with it, because they prized wit and resolve in the women they were with [...]. And they were among the rare men who understood that recognizing somebody else's power does not diminish your own. [...] Well, because these stories [with female protagonists] give people strength.

'Let's Watch A Girl': Whedon, Buffy and Fans in Action
Tanya R. Cochran

These serious answers turn playful as the question continues to come: "'Cause they're hot,' he quips. However, as each successive 'reporter' asks the same question – 'So why do you write these strong women characters?' – and no answer seems sufficient, Whedon the interviewee becomes cheeky.

It's not the repetition that is frustrating; by nature, press junkets are repetitious. The problem is the question itself. Eventually, Whedon raises his voice: 'Why are you even asking me this? [...] How is it possible that this is even a question? [...] Why do you – Why aren't you asking a hundred other guys why they *don't* write strong women characters?' (original emphasis). In this dramatization, Whedon only receives in response to his outburst the same question. He's angry now, but he answers with solemnity. Equality, he says, should not be an idea or future goal. Rather, equality is an ever-present, human necessity: 'Equality is like gravity. We need it to stand on this earth as men and women'. Whedon further insists that the misogyny seen 'in every culture is not a true part of the human condition'. Instead, hatred of women is a weight that disturbs the balance of life on this planet, an 'imbalance [that, like *Buffy*'s vampires] is sucking something out of the soul of every man and woman who's confronted with it'. For this reply, the gala audience erupts in applause, and it seems as if Whedon has delivered his intended message. But he isn't finished. One last time he takes on the part of a reporter who asks, yet again, the question: 'So why do you write these strong female characters?' And Whedon playing Whedon retorts, 'Because you're still asking me that question'.

As mentioned above, Whedon has described his feminism as 'inherent and studied and strongly-felt'. Put another way, his feminism is lived, embodied; who he is affects what he does. Because Whedon holds to feminism, Buffy holds to feminism, even if she herself never uses the word. Though some people continue to argue about whether or not Buffy and *Buffy* are truly feminist, both character and text have incited more than those debates. They have incited the 'peeps' themselves, a community that, with Whedon, believes men and women are inherently equally valuable. Of course, a belief doesn't mean much if it isn't acted on. Significantly, Whedon and his fans do just that: they act.

In May 2007, a year after his Equality Now speech, Whedon posted to *Whedonesque* an entry he provocatively titled 'Let's Watch A Girl Get Beaten To Death'. Utilizing his position, he directed attention toward two events he saw as fundamentally related: the April 2007 stoning to death of a young woman in Bashiqa, Iraq and director Roland Joffé's *Captivity*, which was later released in the United States in July 2007.

Whedon had already publicly campaigned against the advertising of *Captivity*, a movie some critics and viewers have called 'torture porn' for its blend of voyeuristic sexual violence and horror. In fact, he had written an open letter to the Motion Picture Association of America (MPAA) in March a few months prior to 'Let's Watch A Girl' to alert the regulatory organization to the movie's violations of MPAA marketing guidelines. Several billboards in downtown Los Angeles, California, for example, had four close-up, sadistically graphic images of the main character Jennifer Tree accompanied by the words 'Abduction', 'Confinement', 'Torture', and 'Termination'. The title of Whedon's blog – 'Let's Watch A Girl Get Beaten To Death' – clearly refers to *Captivity*'s plot. At the same time, Whedon used the title to share the story of Du'a Khalil Aswad with *Whedoneque* members.

A month before his blog post, a street in northern Iraq had filled with local men who aimed to mete out justice. Seventeen-year-old Aswad had broken her religious community's code of honour by talking to a Muslim young man whom she purportedly planned to run away with and marry. Also, rumours suggested she had converted from Yazidism to Islam. 'Justice' for these alleged 'crimes' involved the men of her faith killing her with their own fists and feet, with stones and cinder blocks. Unfortunately, the meting out of 'justice' by men who deem particular women tainted – whether sexually, religiously or politically – happens every day all over the world. This 'honour' killing, though, was unusual and noted by global news media because it was captured on cell phone videos by multiple men in the crowd, men who did not intervene. The videos were then uploaded to the Internet, went viral, and television news outlets such as CNN broadcast clips until viewers demanded they stop. In the unsteady, blurry footage, one sees, in Whedon's words, 'nothing but red' – the young woman's cerise sweater and crimson blood encircling her crushed head.

'Let's Watch A Girl Get Beaten To Death' references both the fictional Jennifer Tree and the real Du'a Khalil Aswad. Representational and literal violence are related, argued Whedon, and neither can be tolerated. Misogyny, something Whedon claimed he will always address and work against in his texts, pollutes humanity. Echoing the Equality Now speech, Whedon attempted in his remarks about Aswad to address why the hatred of women exists and what should be done about it. He doesn't have all the answers, of course. That's why he has come to the blog. Whedon knows what he has Buffy discover throughout her journey: people need people to change the world. Buffy has her Scoobies. And Whedon has his fans, his community – his 'peeps'.

For the last decade, Whedon has communicated with fans on *Whedonesque*. Because he has a relationship with them, in 'Let's Watch A Girl', Whedon talked familiarly – calling them 'evolved', saying they 'may be way ahead' of him on gender issues, and admitting he couldn't 'contain my despair, for [Aswad], for humanity, for the world we're shaping'. He must speak out, do something. Recognizing his role as a culture maker, he asked fans to do something with him. This move resonates with one Whedon had Buffy make in the seventh season of the television series. When she finally accepts that their enemy, the 'Biggest Bad' she and the Scoobies have ever faced, cannot be defeated by usual means, Buffy realizes she must not simply train and lead the Potential Slayers she has assembled from all over the world – young women who, according to the Slayer mythology, will only receive their own power when Buffy herself, the 'one girl in all the world', dies. She understands that their best chance at victory means breaking

'Let's Watch A Girl': Whedon, Buffy and Fans in Action
Tanya R. Cochran

the ancient spell that allowed only one woman, one Slayer at a time to be supernaturally strong. The now grown-up Scoobies must discover how to transfer Buffy's power to the Potentials. Ultimately, sharing her power multiplies rather than diffuses it and helps save the day – for now – but, more importantly, changes the world – forever.

Mirroring the Scooby Gang's tactics, Whedon broke with Internet-user expectations and hyperlinked 'Let's Watch A Girl Get Beaten to Death' not to cell phone footage of Aswad's stoning but to Equality Now. The world is damaged. Equality Now teaches people to question, stop and prevent that damage. Consequently, partnering with the organization is one way to help. Just being a decent person and feeling bad for Aswad and women like her will never end gendered violence. 'True enlightened activism is the only thing that can save humanity from itself,' Whedon insisted,

All I ask is this: Do something. Try something. Speaking out, showing up, writing a letter, a check, a strongly worded e-mail. Pick a cause – there are few unworthy ones. And nudge yourself past the brink of tacit support to action.

He praised his 'peeps' for what they would have done had they been on that crowded Iraq street. Then Whedon, an expert weaver of words, metaphorically turned the camera on the fan community. Because of technology, they *were* in the crowd, he pointed out. In other words, what they would have done must be what they do.

Feeling always produces a response. Yet not all responses are productive. As Buffy learns in the final episodes of the television series, evil cannot be defeated by wishful thinking, denial or even hope. The only hope is action. Collective action, in the case of *Buffy*. Collective activism, in the case of violence against women.

Within moments, fans began answering the call to activism. In fact, the response was massive: hundreds of follow-up posts comprising nearly 100,000 words of text. But fans didn't just chit-chat; they shared stories and ideas about previous social justice acts and began planning others – from building websites to staging protests, from joining non-profits to hosting fundraising events such as 'Can't Stop the Serenity', annual screenings of Whedon's film *Serenity* (2005) in honour of his June birthday. In the summer of 2006, soon after Whedon's Equality Now speech, the first screening occurred in 46 international cities and raised over $65,000. The next year, a month or so after Whedon's 'Let's Watch A Girl' post, 47 international cities held screenings and raised approximately $106,000. According to the event website, 'Can't Stop the Serenity', started by fan The One True Blx, has to date raised over $600,000 for Equality Now and other charities.

In addition to organizing, fans debated each other – sometimes not so kindly. As Buffy finds out, a fairly long stint as *the* Slayer can breed an arrogantly narrow vision of how to fight evil, a 'Chosen One' brazenness that can aggravate rather than alleviate a problem. In regard to the complexities of gendered violence, efforts to 'save' the world do not necessarily represent the 'true enlightened activism' the world requires (see Trish Salah's 'From Fans to Activists: Popular Feminism Enlists in "The War on Terror"' in the anthology *Contested Imaginaries* [2012]). Importantly, questioning definitions of gendered violence, feminism and feminism itself, gender issues, and the best methods for responding to representational and literal aggression against women was one way fans responded to Whedon's appeal.

Possibly the most moving responses are those in which *Whedonesque* members talked about how their individual investments in themselves and in social justice were set in motion by *Buffy*. Though there are several notable examples, one by QuoterGal stands out:

I will be a feminist until the day I die […] a fiercely protective person to anyone and anything abused by power. But surely one must understand that this gender inequity persists in humanity, and that it expresses itself from the subtlest joke to Du'a Khalil's murder […]. Not coincidentally, one of the things that has given me the greatest hope has been the creation and popularity of *Buffy*. I know it's fiction – which is, by the way, part of our crucial and defining mythologies – and I know it was limited in its reach – but it was popular culture and it has clearly had an important impact. (2007)

Getting even more personal, QuoterGal then admitted that nothing has affected her quite as much as Buffy asking the Potential Slayers in the television series' finale 'Chosen' (Season 7, Episode 22) – the word *one* pointedly absent from that title – 'Are you ready to be strong?' As Buffy's power is magically shared with not only the Potential Slayers she has rallied to fight the First Evil, but also young women everywhere, the camera cuts from scene to scene showing viewers exactly how the world is changing. One of those scenes was particularly powerful for QuoterGal: 'the young girl [raising] her hand to stop her father [from] hitting her – that was me, thirty-five years ago, actually raising my hand against my own father, and that was the first time I had seen my face on TV'. Years later, members of the blog still remark how QuoterGal's words brought them to tears and made them proud to be a part of the *Whedonesque* community. This communal solidarity, recognizing oneself in the other and the other in oneself, represents the 'true enlightened activism' Whedon spoke of.

According to many media scholars, fans keep beloved narratives alive by imagining themselves in them, adopting the style or habits of particular characters, or even imitating the characters they admire most. Essentially, the narrative becomes part of their very being. As QuoterGal's story demonstrates, the phrase 'let's watch a girl' takes on a new dimension if that 'girl' is Buffy, because 'Buffy was a pretty blond girl of whom nothing was expected, who didn't try very hard at anything, and then suddenly became the most powerful person around', Whedon told *Forbes*'s Jeff Bercovici in May 2012: 'That theme, whether it's empowerment or the discovery that one is powerless, that drives everything I do'. Though for years he saw himself as funny yet loser-y Xander, Whedon now thinks otherwise: 'I was Buffy'. A fan could say the same. Many fans could say the same. Through Whedon and *Buffy the Vampire Slayer*, some fans choose, together, to move themselves 'past the brink of tacit support to action', to, as Buffy and the Scoobies did, change the world a lot. ●

GO FURTHER

Extracts/Essays/Articles

'From Fans to Activists: Popular Feminism Enlists in "The War on Terror"'
Trish Salah
In Lisa Taylor and Jasmin Zine (eds.). *Contested Imaginaries: Reading Muslim Women and Muslim Women Reading Back* (New York: Palgrave MacMillan, in press; accepted for publication 2012)

'"Past the brink of tacit support": Fan activism and the Whedonverses'
Tanya Cochran
In Henry Jenkins and Sangita Shresthova (eds.). *Transformative Works and Cultures: 'Transformative Works and Fan Activism'*. 10 (2012), http://journal.transformativeworks. org/index.php/twc/article/view/331/295

'The Purple'.
Joss Whedon
Whedonesque. 9 May 2012, http://whedonesque.com/comments/28797

'"Avenger's" Director Joss Whedon on Trying to Be More Like Buffy'
Jeff Bercovici
Forbes. 3 May 2012, http://www.forbes.com/sites/jeffbercovici/2012/05/03/avengers-director-joss-whedon-on-trying-to-be-more-like-buffy/

'*Fresh Air* Interview with Joss Whedon'
David Bianculli
In David Lavery and Cynthia Burkhead (eds). *Joss Whedon: Conversations* (Jackson: University of Mississippi Press, 2011), pp. 3–13

'The Onion A.V. Club Interview with Joss Whedon (I)'
Tasha Robinson
In David Lavery and Cynthia Burkhead (eds). *Joss Whedon: Conversations*
(Jackson: University of Mississippi Press, 2011), pp. 23–33

'Let's Watch A Girl Get Beaten to Death'
Joss Whedon
Whedonesque. 20 May 2007, http://whedonesque.com/comments/13271

'Joss Whedon Equality Now award acceptance speech'
'On the Road to Equality: Honoring Men on the Front Lines', 15 May 2006.
equalitynowyt. 8 May 2009, http://www.youtube.com/watch?v=QoEZQfTaaEA

'Interview with Joss Whedon'
Shawna Ervin-Gore
Dark Horse Comics. 1 June 2001, http://www.darkhorse.com/

Websites

Equality Now, www.equalitynow.org

Chapter
3

Ficcers and 'Shippers:
A Love Story

Mary Kirby-Diaz

→ STORY-ORIENTED FANS AND SERIES-ORIENTED FANS

Even though the cult TV series, *Buffy the Vampire Slayer* ended a decade ago, fans still rewatch episodes regardless of whether they watch on television, the Internet or DVDs. Internet fans are not a passive audience. Generally more persistent, more committed to their fandoms than were fans before the Internet age, *BtVS* fans still purchase merchandise, attend fan conventions, follow the actors, albeit onto other series, and still create and read fanfiction.

What nourishes these fandoms? What brings in new fans and nourishes the long-time fans of series that are no longer in production?

Answers to these questions may be found in the results of a five-year sociological study of online fans of *Buffy the Vampire Slayer*, completed in 2008. (That study was later expanded to include online fans of *Angel the Series*.) The study focused on fandom as a community, observing what brought fans together, kept them together, and (at times) pulled them apart. Among the study's findings was the observation that the maintenance of a cult TV fandom is related to production of culture and consumption of culture.

Production and consumption are each associated with different types of fans: story-oriented fans and series-oriented fans. While there is some overlap, most fans fall into one of the two categories. Series-oriented fans are involved primarily in the consumption of culture, whereas story-oriented fans are involved primarily in the production of cultural products – fanfiction, fanvidding and fan art, more formally referred to as 'transformative art'.

Series-oriented fans are involved in cultural consumption. The series is the cultural product; the series as a complete package is what fans consume ('cultural consumption'). It's not the relationships or the story that holds them, it's everything: characters, relationships, location, story, mythos, cast, creators – all form the package that series-oriented fans consume. They consume the series by purchasing merchandise that is series-related. Series-oriented fans are the collectors and curators of the fandom. Their treasures are a bonanza: DVDs, character figurines, soundtracks, auctioned props, fan convention memorabilia, bumper stickers, key chains, T-shirts, etc. They accept the story and the characters as seen on television. One fan said, 'It's a television show, it's not up to me to change it'.

Story-oriented fans are producers of culture, producing transformative art primarily in the form of fanfiction and fanvids. Story-oriented fans are transformative artists who view the series' scripts as raw resources to shape to their liking. They seem to have a singular ability to play with plotlines, relationships and characters. They are eager to rework the story, the characters and especially the relationships, to their preferences. Some will even change characters' relationships, locations and time frame (hence the 'Alternate Universe' [or, 'AU'] genre) to recreate the story their way.

Story-oriented fans are also known as 'ficcers' and ''shippers'. Ficcers are fans who write fanfiction; 'shippers are fans of a particular relationship ('ship). It is the story-oriented fan who searches the Internet for fanfiction to read ('shipper); it is the story-oriented fan who writes fanfiction that s/he will post online to share with other fans (ficcer, perhaps also a 'shipper). The terms are not mutually exclusive. Many fanfiction writers are 'shippers; many more online 'shippers read fanfiction than write fanfiction. Indeed, not all ficcers are 'shippers; not all 'shippers are ficcers. 'Shippers need ficcers – and vice versa; one could exist without the other, but their lives would be less fun. 'Shippers need resolution of the characters' relationships they love to follow; ficcers need the

Ficcers and 'Shippers: A Love Story
Mary Kirby-Diaz

reinforcement and gratitude of their readers who 'ship the characters in their stories. Writing Internet fanfiction is an interactive process between 'shipper and ficcer; the fiction writers generally post stories that 'shippers read and comment upon, thus creating a dialogue between the ficcer and the 'shipper.

Both the consumers of culture (series-oriented fans) and producers of culture (story-oriented fans, aka 'shippers and ficcers) believe that they are helping to keep the fandom alive – and they are. One group keeps the series alive by reinforcing their commitment to the series by consuming products that are series-related. The second group – the story-oriented fans – keep the story alive by producing such cultural products as fanfiction and fanvids that continue to enthrall fans whose interest is literary and artistic. Story-oriented fans – ficcers and/or 'shippers – are the social glue that maintains many online fandoms.

A *very* brief guide to ficcers

Fanfiction refers to stories written by fans of a TV series, movie or novel, designed to entertain other fans, written without copyright authorization and without any commercial gain. Fanficcers cannot legally reproduce, sell, perform or display their work, and they cannot write new works based on prior works. In order to prevent breaking copyright law, fanfic writers post a disclaimer (generally at the beginning of each story). Writing fanfiction truly is 'art as a labour of love'. Fanfic writers are amateurs in the sense that their compensation is praise, not money. Compensation is received when the story is commented upon by a reader. According to Melody, a fandom blogger, 'The best fanfic writers become celebrities in their corner of cyberspace, and their works in progress are followed with much enthusiastic anticipation'. (For a sampling of well-written, interesting *BtVS* fanfiction, an appendix of fanfiction recommendations [called 'ficrecs'] follows this article.)

Although copyright laws protect the original owners, in western culture the tradition of telling stories about known characters is strong and ancient. Literary artists have been creating fanfiction for millennia. It happens so frequently that some critics claim that no piece of fiction ever has an original plot. Contemporary Internet fanficcers are the troubadours of fandoms, using the Internet as their medium.

Ficcing (writing fanfiction) can be confusing to outsiders who don't read fanfiction. Some ficcers are also 'shippers who write to express their commitment/enjoyment of a particular 'ship. Others
will say that they don't 'ship when they write fanfic; they're 'just playing in a particular 'ship's sandbox'. Still others will write fanfic to see *if* they can transcend their 'ship to another 'ship – as an artistic challenge. A ficcer might also choose to take the characters or the relationship to another venue – placing the characters in another century, another culture, another time frame, another TV series.

The stereotype of the teenaged girl writing online fanfiction is just that: a stereotype.

It has not been observed in every fandom study; each fandom is unique to some extent. It certainly does not agree with the reality of the fanfiction writers who participated in this study, most of whom were highly-educated females in their mid-/through late-thirties. According to Betsy Gooch, 'Although predominantly believed to be a genre by and for men, science fiction fandom has increasingly been dominated by women for the last half century,' as has been previously observed by Camile Bacon-Smith and Henry Jenkins.

Many fanficcers were career professionals – lawyers, professors, scientists and teachers. Most of the ficcers participating in the study noted at the beginning of this chapter 'shipped at least one 'special' relationship, which they referred to as their OTP (One True Pairing). Still others challenged themselves to write stories without 'ships, and to write stories about many different 'ships.

As with other fandoms, few BtVS fanficcers used their real name; over 90 per cent used an Internet nom de plume. Such cyber names serve a variety of purposes. A fanficcer may want to advertize their 'ship for readers by using a name that reinforces their OTP (One True Pairing), like spikeNdru, or leni_ba. Another fanficcer may want to identify loyalty to a particular character, such as buffyx or spikesheart. Many simply create a new identity that preserves their privacy, like a2zmom, Herself, Miss Murchison, Moscow_watcher, tesla321. Lastly, Internet code names may be chosen because writing fanfiction is a copyright violation.

The fanfic readers who participated in this study were not teenagers: 80 per cent were above the age of 21. They enjoy reading – and 90 per cent of them particularly enjoy reading BtVS fanfiction over the Internet. The reading of fanfiction is a hobby for most 'shippers in the survey, who chose to read Internet fanfiction an average of three hours a week, with a few reading fanfiction for as many as fifteen hours a week. They prefer to read their favourite 'ship(s), and have very definite preferences about the authors, the genre (romance, adventure, hurt/comfort, PWP [Porn Without much Plot], AU [Alternate Universe], etc.), even the ratings (which refer to levels of explicit sex/violence). There was no particular genre that was preferred, though romances, comedies and adventures were ranked more highly.

Because of the Internet's freedom, fanfiction is often edgy – hence the need for ratings to help the reader discern their interest and the 'borders' of their reading enjoyment. Internet fanfiction is often sexually explicit, and certainly more sexually explicit than most of what's available in the authorized novels. Many Internet fanfiction writers – especially those in the BtVS fandom – use ratings borrowed from the movies to denote the age-appropriate level of the story. Many stories that have an R (mature adults) rating will flash a pop-up disclaimer, indicating that the story is targeted to readers of a certain age: 13, 14, 17, For Mature Readers Only (FMRO), or For Mature Adults Only (FMAO). More experienced fanfic readers rely on other fans who've read the story to either recommend it or to review it online. Some writers write only in one rating; others tell the story, then LATER think about the rating.

Ficcers and 'Shippers: A Love Story
Mary Kirby-Diaz

As far as ratings were concerned, 'shippers were not so much seeking online porn as seeking an interesting exposition of characters' feelings or character development, notably lacking in the authorized novels.

For *BtVS* fans, fanfiction is still alive. Not only are fanficcers still writing *BtVS* fanfiction a decade after the series' finale, they are also re-writing the series ending, they are going back to previous episodes and recreating episodes with new characters and new endings. For creative fans and committed 'shippers, fanfiction continues the interaction – the dialogue, the conversation, the story – between the characters and the fan. The sharing of fanfiction – writing it, reading it, expands and deepens the fan community.

Who's 'shipping whom?
I will go down with this 'ship
A 'shipper is a fan who follows a particular *relationship* between two or more characters in a particular TV show. On *BtVS*, for example, 'shippers might follow the major canon relationships like Buffy/Angel or Willow/Tara. Other 'shippers might be interested in non-canonical relationships like Giles/Anya or Wesley/Faith. (The slash line indicates a 'ship.) 'Shippers will often merge the names of the two characters – like Spike/Buffy – into a 'ship name like 'Spuffy', calling themselves 'Spuffies', which is to say, *Spike/Buffy* 'shippers. Most of the online 'shippers in the study read fanfiction; some not only read fanfiction, they wrote fanfiction for (other) online 'shippers to read. 'Shippers often reported that they watched *BtVS* to follow their favourite 'ship (relationship). Some 'shippers read fanfiction; some don't. Those who do read fanfiction often admit that reading fanfiction becomes '... a way of life', or 'a hobby'. More than one fan reported that 'fanfic's become an addiction'.

Buffy fans from Australia, Brazil, Canada, Finland, France, Germany, Holland, Ireland, Italy, Malaysia, New Zealand, Peru, Russia, Scotland, Sweden, Turkey, the United States, the United Kingdom and Wales, responded to the study's three online surveys during the late summer/early autumn, 2003. The responses were overwhelming: over one hundred participants provided over 5,000 responses about fanfiction, ficcers and 'ships.

Defying the stereotype of the female high-school teen fan, most online *BtVS* 'shippers were revealed to be single females, highly educated career professionals or college/graduate students 21 to 40 years of age. In fact, nearly three-fourths of them graduate or professional degrees, and about one-third were mothers, mostly of young children under ten years of age.

Both *Buffy* and *Angel* had a broad array of relationships for fans to follow: the *BtVS* fans had a LOT of 'ships; the 108 participants in that survey listed 53 'ships, including Buffy's three major on-screen relationships: (Buffy/Angel, Buffy/Riley and Buffy/Spike) and such non-screen 'ships as Giles/Anya and Spike/Xander. Indeed, many participants identified 'ships that weren't even included in the original study, such as Giles/Buffy and Angel/Oz. Early *BtVS* seasons encouraged 'shippers for Xander/Cordelia and Willow/Oz, only to create subsequent 'ships for Xander/Anya and Willow/Tara.

As the show's writers created new relationships for their characters, 'shipper wars – heated exchanges between 'shippers of rival 'ships (Buffy/Angel and Buffy/Spike, for example) – dotted both series. During the seven-season run of *BtVS* three major 'ship schisms emerged: Buffy/Angel, Buffy/Spike and Spike/Angel. The last 'ship became canon in *Angel the Series*' final season.

There's one category of 'shippers that is key: the 'shippers who follow their One True Pairing (OTP). OTP is a term that identifies the 'shipper's most favourite 'ship (pairing). 'Shippers use the term OTP to denote that *this* pairing belongs together forever. The 'shippers in the study asserted that they may enjoy reading stories about other 'ships, or stories without a 'ship (called 'genfic' for 'general story', no 'ship), but the stories they most enjoy are those about their OTP. In all of the online surveys, the fans' most popular *BtVS* OTPs, in descending order were: Buffy/Spike, Buffy/Angel, Angel/Spike, Spike/Xander. Over half of the fans who replied to the survey were Buffy/Spike fans, while slightly more than one-third each 'shipped Buffy/Angel and Angel/Spike. Other popular 'ships that *BtVS* fans enjoyed reading about, but did not consider to be their OTP, in descending order, included Willow/Tara, Spike/Drusilla, Willow/Oz, Xander/Cordelia and Angel/Darla.

Angel/Spike and Buffy/Spike 'shippers particularly enjoy reading the ways in which ficcers wrote about the chemistry between the characters – banter, fighting together against a common enemy and fighting with/against each other. Spangel and Spuffie 'shippers often complained about the authorized novels which are written for the Young Adult reader.

Interestingly, 'shippers of different 'ships often reported the same reasons for their attraction to a particular 'ship. For example, Angel/Buffy 'shippers reported that they are attracted to the chemistry between the actors and feel that the love between Angel and Buffy is formidable. They discussed the significance of the character's love – not sexual attraction – as the key to the importance of the Buffy/Angel relationship. Many compared the Buffy/Angel love story to Romeo and Juliet, in that Buffy and Angel are enemies who transcend their differences through mutual respect and love. Ironically, many Buffy/Spike 'shippers used the same reasons for their attachment to that 'ship.

Who are the *BtVS* 'shippers? What variables, as sociologists say, do they share? Are there variables that are more likely to describe each 'ship? Are age, gender, marital status, occupation, important in identifying possible 'shippers? The average age of each 'shipper is somewhat associated with which 'ship a fan may follow. When it comes to 'ship, age matters: the oldest 'shippers were usually Spangels; the youngest were usually Buffy/Angel 'shippers. (These are statistical generalities, since some Spangels were older teens and some Buffy/Angel 'shippers were in their forties.)

Spike/Buffy 'shippers
The most popular 'ship in the *BtVS* study was Spike/Buffy, and the Spuffies, have the

Ficcers and 'Shippers: A Love Story
Mary Kirby-Diaz

money, and education to keep it afloat. They were likely to be in their mid-30s, married, highly-educated with BA or other professional degrees. About one-third of the Buffy/ Spike 'shippers were parents – more than for any other 'ship studied. These 'shippers have completely integrated the reading of fanfiction into their lives.

Spuffies read fanfic, making it a part of their daily lives by printing out the fanfic and taking it everywhere they go to read as they wait somewhere, with their lunch, on the train or subway, sitting in the park. Neglected by authorized novelizations, they re-inforce their 'ship by gobbling up Internet fanfiction: long or short, fluffy or dramatic, romantic or funny; they read it all.

Philosophically, they don't believe in an idealized love. They see love between two people as 'the end product of their history' as one participant related. Spuffies like the progression of Buffy and Spike from enemies to 'frenemy' to lovers, to trusting friends, to allies, and finally, back to lovers. As one participant wrote:

Ah, Buffy and Spike – I love the energy between these two, the fact that everything in the world says they shouldn't be together and tries to tear them apart – and yet, they always seem to be drawn to one another, whether they are enemies, lovers or allies. This is grand passion with all the fire and angst, but there's a core of something else there as well, of understanding and respect.

Buffy/Angel 'shippers
Buffy/Angel 'shippers are usually single young females. Their average age was 23. More than half were college students, a few were still in high school. Less than a third were married; only one was a parent. Being mostly students, it's not surprising that they are not affluent. Some had jobs, usually part-time.

The Young Adult reader is the target audience for the authorized *BtVS* fanfiction. Over 100 novels, as well as thousands of online fanfiction are at their disposal – which is a major advantage in being a Buffy/Angel 'shipper. Accessibility to these novels is a key to sustaining the 'ship as well as the fandom. In contrast, the Spuffy 'shipper may be an older, more highly-educated career professional, but she must use the Internet to access the fanfiction she desires to read, because it is not available anywhere else.

The Buffy/Angel 'shipper spends about eight hours a week reading fanfiction, and they do seek out Internet fanfiction for those NC-17 stories they can't find in the novels. Despite this, their reading habits are usually conservative – no slash ('slash' refers to same sex pairings), heterosexual (except for Willow/Tara, which is canon), no multiple-partners, no kinky sex. They want 'a good romance with lots of UST' (unresolved sexual tension). Should the two characters have sex, it's post-series, with Angel having earned his Shanshu or having had Willow cast a spell to protect Buffy. Unlike the older Spuffy, they don't print out their fanfic to read offline; the younger B/A (Buffy/Angel) 'shipper is accustomed to high-tech reading.

Fig.1: ©Andrea Chapman

Fig.2: ©Susan Moore

Not deterred by Buffy's *affaires d'amour* with Riley and Spike, and Angel's with Darla, and on *Angel the Series* with Cordelia and Nina, Buffy and Angel's love for each other is a 'forever' love that continues, despite space and time; other loves are transient in comparison. Even Joss Whedon's declaration, 'Buffy loves *both* Angel *and* Spike, but has moved on,' is fairly meaningless in the glow of a love that represents the (generally) younger segment of 'shippers. One participant wrote, 'Angel's affairs with Darla and Cordelia don't mean anything; neither does Buffy's interest in Spike and Riley. Angel is her true love and Buffy is his'. Buffy/Angel 'shippers believe in an ideal, a love between soul mates that withstands the occasional *affaire* with another character.

Interestingly, Buffy/Angel 'shippers often mentioned Spike/Dru as their second favourite 'ship to read about. This makes sense: if Spike is 'shipping Dru, he won't be 'shipping Buffy! Several B/A 'shippers also mentioned Spike/Dawn as one of their favourite 'ships – they see analogies between the 'ages' of Spike and Angel when each first met Dawn and Buffy. One participant reported, 'Buffy started to date Angel when she was sixteen – the same age as Dawn in season seven'.

Spike/Angel 'shippers

'Spangel', aka, Spike/Angel, was the third most popular 'ship reported in the study. Age-wise, the average Spangel 'shipper was well-educated, more likely to be single than married, 32 years old. They are attracted to the chemistry between the characters, the bantering, and the history of their relationship as vampires, as sire and younger vampire.

Spangels are voracious readers, spending about sixteen hours a week reading fanfiction straight off the Internet. They'll read any genre, any length, and they want their reading steamy, hot and sexy. Few Spangels read any fanfiction below a rating of Mature Adult, R or FMAO (For Mature Adults Only).

At sixteen hours of reading weekly, every week, one may ask how *much* fanfiction is on the Internet. The answer: A LOT. A Google search conducted in late May 2012 revealed almost 25,000 hits for Spike/Angel fanfiction – nearly a decade after both series ended. Like the famously shipped Captain James T. Kirk and Mr Spock (Kirk/Spock) of *Star Trek* (Gene Roddenberry, 1966-69) fandom, Spike/Angel lives on in 'shippers' hearts.

Spike/Xander 'shippers

Spanders were the fourth most popular 'ship in this study. Their average age is 31, and they are more likely to be the least educated of the four most popular groups of 'shippers, earning high school diplomas rather than college degrees. They're more likely to be single, less likely to be parents.

They are attracted to the Spike/Xander relationship because: 'They're [Xander and Spike] both nerds'. 'They're both outsiders'. 'They are perfect for each other'. 'They complement each other'. 'I like their banter'. 'They each have lots of emotional baggage and they're good for each other'. 'They have similar personalities and traits'.

Ficcers and 'Shippers: A Love Story
Mary Kirby-Diaz

Like the other 'shippers in this study, Spanders love to read fanfiction about their OTP; indeed, 'shippers of all OTPs often recommend Spander fanfic as among their favourite stories. Spander 'shippers prefer long NC-17 rated stories, regardless of genre.

Conclusion
Since the study's completion, subsequent random observations of the online partici- pants' reading, writing and 'shipping loyalties indicate that little change has taken place. For example, participants who 'shipped Buffy/Spike still 'ship Buffy/Spike – despite hav- ing moved to other fandoms, and other 'ships. One Internet site (see Appendix below), 'The Sunnydale Herald', posts new/*BtVS* fanfiction almost every day.

Appendix
This is a sampling of fanfiction for fans new to reading fanfiction. It's all classic – that is, written prior to December 2008. All links intact as of 31 May 2012. Too shy to leave a comment at the ficcers' website? You can send comments to me at mary.kirby-diaz@ farmingdale.edu. I'd love to read your comments, and will be happy to pass them onto the ficcers.

Pre-series
'Wild Demonic Fauna' by Peasant, http://peasant.notanothersite.com/fiction/wildde- monicfauna.html
'Bag of Bones' by Roz Kaveney, http://glamourousrags.dymphna.net/bedofbones.html
'Kiss Me Deadly' by Shannon, http://web.archive.org/web/20031209223550/http:// www.tar-xvf.net/shannon/fic/kissmedeadly/index.html

Non-'ship character studies
Buffy: Rob Sorenson, 'Schoolbus Rock',
http://www.soulfulspike.com/schoolbusrock.htm
Angel: Cas, 'The Hobo', http://web.archive.org/web/20050312013435/http://www. dawnshadows.com/darkness/hobo/hobo.htm
Spike: cagd, 'Wendy', http://www.fanfiction.net/s/2518820/1/Wendy
Cordelia: Jennifer Oksana, 'Reclamation', http://silverlake.dymphna.net/jeno-recla- mation.html

'Ships
Spike/Buffy: anaross, 'My Life Closed Twice',
http://www.athenewolfe.com/justrewards/viewstory.php?sid=577
Buffy/Angel: Trixie Firecracker, 'The Life Before Her Eyes',
http://www.octavesoftheheart.com/sublime/life.htm
Spike/Angel: Romany, 'His Body a Boat',

http://www.octavesoftheheart.com/romany/bodyisaboat.htm
Spike/Xander: Tesla, 'Magnetism',
http://www.wonderhorse.net/authorspgs/tesla/magnetism.htm
Spike/Dru: Indri, 'Honeymoon', http://notanothersite.com/indri/honeymoon.html

Genfic
Ensemble: Marcus L. Rowland, 'Legend', http://bbfarchive.dbfandom.com/archive/1/
legend.html

AU (Alternate Universe)
BtVS/AtS: Tesla, 'The S Curve', http://tesla321.livejournal.com/153039.html

Crossover
BtVS/West Wing: Spikewriter, 'Just Another Meeting', http://spikewriter.livejournal.
com/295406.html

Archives
'All About Spike', http://www.allaboutspike.com/
'Angel Book of Days', http://archiveofourown.org/tags/Angel%20Book%20of%20
Days%20Challenge/works
and http://archiveofourown.org/collections/Angel_Book_of_Days
'Archive of Our Own', http://archiveofourown.org/tags/Jossverse/works
'Better Buffy Fiction Archive', http://bbfarchive.dbfandom.com/
'Buffy Fiction Archive', http://archive.shriftweb.org/
'Chosen Fics', http://www.chosenfics.com/cf/links.html
'Octaves of the Heart', http://www.octavesoftheheart.com/
'PhantasMagoria', http://fantas-magoria.livejournal.com/201032.html
'Scribes of Angel', http://www.scribes.darkstarfic.com/
'The Sunnydale Herald', http://su-herald.livejournal.com/
'Twisting the Hellmouth: Crossovers', http://www.tthfanfic.org/

Fanficcers' versions of extended series
Each has at least 22 episodes (chapters):
Season 6: 'No Limits', http://-nolimits.livejournal.com/
Season 8/+ *BtVS*: 'Project Paranormal', http://project.darkstarfic.com/index.php
Season 6: 'Spike on his own: Soul Survivor',
http://www.newsgarden.org/soulsurvivor/ss.shtml
Season 9/+ *BtVS*: 'Giles, Willow, Faith, Kennedy, Andrew, Xander, and of course, Buffy:
The Watcher's Council', http://www.thewatcherscouncil.net/ ●

Ficcers and 'Shippers: A Love Story
Mary Kirby-Diaz

~~~~~~~~~

GO FURTHER

Books

Buffy and Angel Conquer the Internet: Essays on Online Fandom
Mary Kirby-Diaz
(North Carloina: McFarland Press, 2010)

Cyberspaces of Their Own: Female Fandoms Online
Rhiannon Bury
(New York: Peter Lang, 2005)

Seven Seasons of 'Buffy': Science Fiction and Fantasy Writers Discuss Their Favorite Television Show
Glenn Yeffeth
(Dallas, TX: Benbella Books, 2003)

Fan Cultures
Matt Hills
(London: Routledge, 2002)

Theorizing Fandom: Fans, Subculture, and Identity
Eds Cheryl Harris and Alison Alexander
(Cresskill, NJ: Hampton Press, Inc., 1998)

Textual Poachers: Television Fans And Participatory Culture
Henry Jenkins
(NY: Routledge, 1992)

Enterprising Women: Television Fandom and the Creation of Popular Myth
Camille Bacon-Smith
(Philadelphia: University of Pennsylvania Press, 1992)

The Adoring Audience: Fan Culture and Popular Media
Ed. Lisa Lewis
(London: Routledge, 1992)

Extracts/Essays/Articles

'The Fandom Project'
Mary Kirby-Diaz
In Patricia Epee (ed.). *For the Love of Angel* (in press).

'Buffy the Vampire Slayer without Joss Whedon? That's Been Going on for Years'
Roz Kaveney
In *The Guardian*. 24 November 2010, http://bit.ly/113Hdpd

'The Fandom Project: What Makes a Fandom Run? Characters, 'Ships, Fics, and Fancons'
Mary Kirby-Diaz
Presented at the *North East Popular Culture Association Conference*. Nashua College, Nashua. 27–28 October 2006.

'The Fandom Project: What Makes a Fandom Run – 'Ships, Fanfiction, Plot Devices, Favorite Characters and FanCons'
Mary Kirby-Diaz
In the *International Journal of the Humanities*. 3: 4 (2006), pp. 256–65.

'The Fandom Project: What Keeps a Fandom Afloat? Report Two: 'Ships'
Mary Kirby-Diaz
Presented at the *Slayage Conference on the Whedonverses*. Barnesville, GA, 25–28 May 2006.

'Fan Readings of Sex and Violence on Buffy the Vampire Slayer'
Dawn Heinecken
In *Slayage: The Journal of the Whedon Studies Association Vol 3.3-4*: Heinecken. (2004), http://slayageonline.com/essays/slayage11_12/Heinecken.htm.

'Community From Hell'
Asim Ali
Presented at the *Slayage Conference on the Whedonverses*. Nashville, TN, 27-30 May 2004.

'Buffy, Angel, and Virtual Communities'
Mary Kirby-Diaz
Presented at the *Popular Culture Association Conference*. San Antonio, TX April 2004.

'Buffy, Angel, and the Creation of Virtual Communities'
Mary Kirby-Diaz
Presented at the *Slayage Conference on the Whedonverses*, Nashville, TN, 27-30 May 2004.

Ficcers and 'Shippers: A Love Story
Mary Kirby-Diaz

'Buffy Brings Fans Together'
Denise Grollmus
In *The Beacon Journal*. 21 July 2003.
Edition: 1StARS, Section B, Page B1
Issue 98 of the 165th year

'War of the Worlds: Richard Chaves, Paul Ironhorse, and the Female Fan Community'.
Cinda Gillilan
In Cheryl Harris and Alison Alexander (eds). *Theorizing Fandom: Fans, Subculture, and Identity* (NJ: Hampton Press, Inc., 1998), pp. 179–99.

'Real and Ideal Others in Romantic Relationships: Is Four a Crowd?'
Robert Sternberg
In *Journal of Personality and Social Psychology*, 49 (1985), pp. 1589–96.

'Television's Afterlife (angel Mention)'
Marlene Arpe
samedi 22 mai 2004, par Webmaster
website: Whedoninfo
http://www.whedon.info/article.php3?id_article=4722.

'The Watcher: The Unlimited Playgrounds of Fanfiction'
Amy Berner
website: Octaves of the Heart
http://www.octavesoftheheart.com/octaves/amy.htm.

'Confessions of a Spikeoholic'
Melody
lundi 25 août 2003, par Webmaster
website: Whedoninfo
http://www.whedon.info/Confessions-of-a-Spikeoholic.html.

'Fandom Sociology: The Mechanics Behind the Beast'
Princess Twilight
website: Octaves of the Heart
http://www.octavesoftheheart.com/octaves/fandom.htm.

'Bite Me, Professor'
Ian Shuttleworth

vendredi 12 septembre 2003, par Webmaster
website: Whedoninfo
http://www.whedon.info/article.php3?id_article=1567.

'Why Don't Men Write Fanfiction?'
Kyla Gorman
USC Cinematic Arts: Interactive Media Division
29 October 2009
http://interactive.usc.edu/2009/10/29/why-dont-men-write-fanfiction/.

'Quotes About Fanfiction' [9 Quotes]
Joss Whedon
website: good reads
http://www.goodreads.com/quotes/show_tag?id=fanfiction.

'Twoforjoy Comments on I Am Joss Whedon'
Joss Whedon
10 April 2012
website: reddit.com
http://www.reddit.com/r/IAmA/comments/s2uh1/i_am_joss_whedon_ama/c4amrcn.

'The Confessions of a Semi-Successful Fanfic Writer'
Cordelia Lear
This is from a now-defunct website, teevee.org, posted originally on 1 April 2004,
accessed via a web archive site.
http://web.archive.org/web/20070402230552/http://www.teevee.org/
archive/2004/04/01/arts-fanfic.html
[Ed. Note: This is a parody of fanfic writers.]

'Fan the Flames'
Yuki-onna
10 May 2010
http://yuki-onna.livejournal.com/582169.html. (New URL for that site: http://
catvalente.livejournal.com/582169.html)

Films and Television

It's Never Too Late to Become a Buffy Fan, Kiss Me Jane, dir. (Ottawa: KMJ Productions, 2004)

Fan Appreciation no.1
Nikki Stafford of the Great *Buffy* Rewatch

Nikki Stafford is an editor, and author – having published companion guides to *Xena*, *Buffy the Vampire Slayer*, *Angel*, *Alias* and *Lost* through ECW Press. She blogs at her website, *Nik at Nite*, where she organized 'The Great *Buffy* Rewatch of 2011'. Stafford received a coveted 'Mr Pointy' award at the *Fifth Biennial Slayage Conference on the Whedonverses* in recognition of her contributions to furthering *Buffy* studies.

Jennifer K. Stuller (JKS): *You wrote the first guide to* Buffy *in* Bite Me!: Sarah Michelle Gellar and 'Buffy the Vampire Slayer' (ECW, 1998); *later* Bite Me!: The Chosen Edition: The Unofficial Guide to 'Buffy The Vampire Slayer' [Seven Seasons One Book] (ECW, 2007). *What drew you to the series, and what was it about the show that you recognized as unique so early on – especially unique enough to write and publish a guide when the series was so young?*

Nikki Stafford (NS): I had just finished my first book on *Xena: Warrior Princess*, and when my publisher had signed me up to do it, he'd expected what was typical of episode guides at the time: title of the episode, plot synopsis and some pull-out quotes of funny bits. But as I was in the process of finishing up my Master's degree in English literature, I didn't want to write a book like that. I thought, if you're writing an essay on a particular book, you don't simply regurgitate the plot and hand that in to your professor; you instead assume the professor has read the book already, and you analyse it. And so that's how I decided to approach the episode guide for *Xena*. I would write about the actual stories of the Greek gods and tie them into the episodes, talk about the plot developments, string episode arcs together and critique whether or not they were working, and I'd ignore plot summary altogether. And it worked: when the book came out, it was a big success and sold out almost immediately.

So for my next book, I wanted to find a show where I could write about something more beyond the plot summary. *Buffy* seemed the perfect fit: I could write about the folklore surrounding vampires, werewolves, ghosts, Wiccans and every other creature that showed up week-to-week. I had only seen a couple of episodes, but knew this was what I wanted to write about. So I contacted some fans, got my hands on every episode that had aired up to that point (the show was currently on hiatus between 'Killed by Death' and 'I Only Have Eyes for You') and watched them all in a couple of days. And I was completely hooked and *thrilled* I'd chosen this show to write on. I wrote the first edition in under three months.

JKS: *You are a presence at your blog and website,* Nik at Nite, *where you interact with fans of popular culture (quite notably fans of* Lost, *for which you wrote several series guides). Tell us about your experience with BtVS fandom on the Internet, and about fan communities found and cultivated while presenting and participating at several Slayage Conferences. Are you surprised that passion for the series can be just as strong in a scholarly space as an online one?*

NS: Not at all. I originally approached the series in a scholarly fashion, so it seemed like a natural fit to me. The fandom in the *Xena* culture was very strong: 'Xenites' were composed of very specific demographics of people who gravitated to the character of Xena – strong, domineering, incredibly smart, feminist, possibly lesbian – or to the character of her sidekick, Gabrielle – a poet, funny, beautiful, intelligent, artsy, optimistic, possibly lesbian. The community was one that was tight-knit (I saw a lot of people meet online and enter serious relationships through their shared interest in the show) and cohesive, and there were fan meet-ups everywhere. I was firmly entrenched in the community, 'filking', and going to the fan conventions and meeting as many people as I could.

The *Buffy* fandom was entirely different. When the show was in its early period, the fandom consisted of a lot of teenagers. Everyone was putting up websites and finding their niches – they were identifying with various characters, writing fanfiction, etc. – and most of the devoted fans were hanging out at 'The Bronze', this fantastic forum the WB had put up where you could talk about *Buffy* all day long, and the actors and writers on the show would actually come on and participate in the conversations. I didn't have a lot of time to be on 'The Bronze' as much as I wanted to, and on mailing lists people didn't want to talk about the show as in-depth as I wanted to; the conversations mostly veered to whether Buffy should be with Angel or Spike, who was the hottest on the show, and, later, the relationships between many of the other characters. I found a group of *Buffy* fans here in Toronto that met monthly and joined them, and they were the first great group of *Buffy* fans that I found in the beginning.

When I discovered that a group of academics were talking about the show the way I wanted to, I was thrilled. That wasn't until after I'd finished the second edition of my book, which came out in 2002 and covered up to Season 6, but it was nice to see that there existed a group of scholars who were as interested in the minutiae of *BtVS* as I was. I first heard about them when I appeared on a TV talk show here in Toronto on a specialty channel called BookTelevision. I was part of a panel of people to discuss

BtVS, and it was held shortly after 'Once More With Feeling' had aired. Host and Canadian personality Daniel Richler had me on as the expert from the fan side of things, alongside another woman who was a Ph.D. candidate who had been to the first *Buffy* conference in East Anglia, and a man who was a musical expert. The woman who'd been to East Anglia told us all about the conference, and I was thrilled to hear there was such a thing and that people had actually gathered in such a large group to discuss my favourite thing. (Even though the woman barely spoke to me, and kept waving the back of her hand at me as if willing me to go away.) The next time I heard about *Slayage* was when I was invited to the 2004 conference as a keynote, but I was very pregnant at the time and couldn't come. When I was invited again in 2008, I happily said yes. I was nervous about the reception I'd get there (especially after getting the cold shoulder from the East Anglia scholar) but I couldn't have been more wrong. What a wonderful group of people. Finally I'd found the camaraderie and synchronicity that I had been looking for in *Buffy* fandom.

JKS: *What is it about* Buffy *that brings people together, be it online, or in real life?*

NS: I think it's because the show portrayed situations that so many of us can relate to. As I've said many times, name a high school that *wasn't* located on a hellmouth: high school is a terrible, awful, no good, very bad place, and many people have terrible memories of it. Those of us who fell into the high school categories of either freak or geek (or both) all think that the jocks and cheerleaders probably look back on high school as the golden years, but as 'Earshot' demonstrated, even they were going through difficult times. *Buffy* used the monsters as metaphors for the angst and personal demons that each one of us is forced to conquer as we find our way through high school, move out into the real world and try to find our place in it, lose friends, experience the deaths of loved ones. In seven years, we became strongly attached to these characters as if they were our own friends and family, and that's a testament to how well the show was both written and acted.

Now, almost a decade after the show went off the air, new viewers are still coming to it, and while certain references may feel a little dated, and the technology is woefully ancient (imagine how different things would have been for our heroes with cellphones and texting and social media), the underlying issues are timeless. Ask a fan who they identify with most on the show, and they can usually name a character instantly. And often, they'll add, 'Although, when I watched the series recently I found I identified with a different character ...'

And that's the thing about *Buffy*: while on first viewing it seemed to be a show that made us nostalgic for our high school years (and I mean nostalgic in the sense of looking back and thinking, 'Never in a million years would I want to return to those days'), the show took a hard look at adulthood as well. Through Giles and Joyce and Spike and Angel, we saw the perils of growing up, and the choices that have to be made. It was clear that bullying exists even after high school, whether in the workplace or among friends. Giles finds love and ends up alone more than once on the show; Joyce's husband has left her for his younger secretary and when she finally finds someone to connect with, she dies immediately after their first date. Both face the difficulty of being parents, of always making mistakes while trying to do the right thing.

Buffy the Vampire Slayer was an extraordinary show about youth, age, friends, family, authority, responsibility, being alive while dead inside (literally with the vampires, and metaphorically with Buffy in Season 6), staying alive while others die, personal demons, love and hope. And those are all things everyone can relate to.

JKS: *You had toyed with the idea of a* Buffy *rewatch, but were overwhelmed by the prospect of recapping 144 episodes on your own and so recruited academics, scholars, novelists, poets, pop culture bloggers other writers of TV companion guides, and even a sports writer. How did you go about selecting such a diverse set of contributors?*

NS: The Rewatch was always conceived as something that would involve a lot of people. I could have handled it on my own (and in the end I did end up watching 144 episodes and writing something on them every week), but for me the purpose of the Rewatch was manifold: I had met all of these wonderful Whedon scholars at *Slayage*, and I wanted to show off their many talents and vast knowledge to the thousands of readers on my blog, many of whom had no idea that pop culture academia even existed. But also, I wanted to demonstrate that bloggers and episode guide writers could analyse and interpret shows in a different way, using different language. (I'll talk more about that in question 7.) And finally, I wanted to illustrate that *Buffy* is something that appeals across many demographics, so I recruited the academics and bloggers, but also novelists, poets, journalists, a golf writer, episode guide authors, a television producer and fans, to show as many different perspectives and approaches as I possibly could. I was the anchor, writing something week after week, but everyone else kept it unique and interesting and changed up the tone week after week.

JKS: *Why do you think* Buffy *lends itself to so many interpretations from different disciplines and points of view?*

NS: I think, as I mentioned earlier, it's the way that *Buffy* just touches a universal nerve. If people watching the show can relate to it, then they'll naturally relate it to their disciplines. I've seen papers that explore *Buffy* through literary analysis, scientific research, an anthropological lens, historical perspective – because *Buffy* is so relatable, the possibilities for ways to study it are endless.

JKS: *What do repeat viewings of* Buffy *offer viewers/readers of pop culture? And what can a viewer (newbie, or addict) gain from watching from Episode 1 straight through to 144?*

NS: A first viewing, as with any show, is pure entertainment. Once you know what's going to happen, you can begin to look for different things. I think repeat viewings of *Buffy* are essential, because there are so many new surprises waiting in every episode. People have asked me how many times I've seen the series. Occasionally I'll watch an episode on its own (when I turn on the TV and find an episode of *Buffy*, I find it very hard to turn away), but typically I watch the series from beginning to end. Unlike many *Buffy* viewers, I was watching it almost from the beginning, and had to wait a week (or, in the case of summers, several months) to see the next episode, whereas now people can devour the series very quickly. So I've seen the earlier seasons several more times than the later ones, but all the way through I've seen it over ten times. And I'm still finding things I've missed before.

JKS: *At the* Fourth Biennial Slayage Conference on the Whedonverses, *you co-presented a Banquet Keynote with Dr Matthew Pateman with the fabulously lengthy title, '"Oh, wouldn't it be tragic if you were here being kinda silly with your comically paralysed sister while Willow was dying?" or "Excellent. Now. Do we suspect that there may be some connection between Ben and Glory?": The tragi-comic/comic-tragic methods of miscommunication in Buffy'. Famously known in certain circles (aka 'The Whedon Studies Association') as 'The Great Stafford vs Pateman rhetori-*

cal battle of 2010' (a title which I just completely made up) the presentation, more a performance really, explored the occasionally frustrating relationship between the 'aca-fan' and the 'scholar-fan'. How did you see both these positions being reflected in the Buffy *rewatch? And how much do they really overlap?*

NS: That was so much fun to do! And Matthew Pateman was a really great sport about it. The presentation originated from an incident at the *Third Biennial Slayage Conference*. I was the banquet keynote speaker, and just as I was about to go up, the person introducing me said, 'While all of *us* are scholar-fans, Nikki is a fan-scholar'. While I didn't know exactly what that meant yet, what I did know was that it declared me as being different from everyone else in the room, and not in a good way. Afterwards, someone came up to me and asked me how I felt being called a fan-scholar, and I asked her what that meant. She explained that the term was coined by an academic who studies fandom, named Matt Hills, and that a scholar-fan is someone who is identified as an academic first, a fan second; a fan-scholar is the opposite.

After the conference, the more I thought about that difference, the more it started to grate on me. I'd met Pateman at that conference and we discussed the difference between the two a lot afterwards. He had also written a book on *Buffy*, and what I found interesting is that he watched the show first, and after it finished decided to write a book on it. His book came out in 2006. I, on the other hand, had been signed to write my book on *Buffy* after I'd only seen a couple of episodes. So when I first started watching the show seriously, it was already with an eye to writing on it (the first edition of my book came out in 1998). In that sense, our approaches would suggest that I was actually the scholar-fan (since I knew I was studying it before I liked it), and he was the fan-scholar.

Of course, if you read our books you'd know his is far more academic than mine, so those terms just don't fit, which made them even more troublesome. In our many discussions, we discussed why there has to be a divide between the two: aren't bloggers dissecting and analysing the series and bringing a new perspective to it for fans, just as the academics are? Why should we be handed a term that basically pats us on the head in a patronizing fashion and says, 'Oh, of *course* you are important to pop culture studies. But, you know, you're not actually an *academic* so we can't say you're equally important, right?' (Not that any scholar at *Slayage* has ever made me feel this way; it's the categories that do.) So we came up with the idea of exploring an argument about whether *Buffy* is a drama tinged with comedy (my thesis) or a comedy with some drama in it (Pateman's thesis) but approaching it as if he's the pompous academic and I'm the slang-slinging blogger. We communicated our arguments in completely different ways (often pretending we simply couldn't understand the other one), yet by the end of the presentation, working together, we had offered an argument for both sides that the audience had been able to follow. (My side won. That's my story and I'm sticking to it.)

So, when it came to the Rewatch, I wanted to do the same thing. I wanted to show, as I mentioned earlier, that non-academics and academics can stand side by side, both offering different ways of looking at a show that we all love. One thing I want to add here is that, while *Buffy* is certainly a show worthy of study, as so many fantastic Whedon scholars have shown, it's a show with a lot of heart. And that's where we bloggers come in: we can talk about the moments that pulled our heartstrings and look at the human side of everything, without having to bring it around to a thesis. We can be descriptive without arguing a point. And the *Buffy* Rewatch allowed for the in-depth and fascinating scholarly look at the show to stand side-by-side with the emotional reaction. While the Rewatch garnered such a positive reaction, one of the most memorable entries resulted when I asked a friend of mine, who had lost her father ten years ago, to write about what it is like watching 'The Body' having gone through the death of a parent. It's a piece I still can't read without getting choked up, and while we can discuss the success of that episode based on the writing, the acting, the lack of music, the *mise-en-scène*, the speeches, the silence … none of that is as powerful as hearing someone talk about how she was able to watch this episode of television and come to terms with the saddest moment of her life.

And one last note on the fan-scholar/scholar-fan dichotomy: I doubt any of the *Slayage* scholars would say they're a fan of *Buffy* second, and see it primarily as a thing to be studied. They'd all identify as fan-scholars when it comes to the Whedonverse.

JKS: *As the watch evolved, decisions were made regarding the idea of 'spoiling' vs 'non-spoiling' and whether or not to include episodes of* Angel the Series *in the rewatch, as part of the extended* Buffyverse?

NS: Yes, it was the one thing I hadn't considered going into the Rewatch: if I'm trying to recruit many of the readers of my *Lost* blog to finally check out this *Buffy* thing I've been talking about for years, how do we discuss the early episodes without mentioning anything that might spoil the future?

Luckily, the discussions happened in the very first week, and I realized the best option would be to split every week into two posts: the spoiler-free one, and the spoiler one. After a few weeks we'd all settled into a routine: the contributors could put spoilers in their writing, and I'll hide it from the newbies, but the experienced viewers could simply highlight a seemingly blank section and it would magically appear. And if commenters wanted to have a spoilery discussion in the comments section, they would simply jump to the other post and do it there. It worked beautifully. When we approached Season 4, I had to make a decision about what to do with *Angel*, and I decided I wouldn't do a full *Angel* Rewatch, but instead would mention what episodes appeared concurrently with that week's episodes of *Buffy*, and I would usually say a few words about the episodes and open up the discussions so people could talk about *Angel* in the comments section. It worked: many of the new viewers were watching *Angel* along with us, and if they had any questions about the episodes, they could ask them in the comments and one of us would answer for them.

JKS: *During the Rewatch you remarked how now that you have your own children, your thinking towards Joyce Summers's parenting had changed. Can you say more about that? And were there any other changes in perspective that may have been surprising? Was there anything you remembered liking before, but didn't upon repeat viewing? (i.e. Xander being kind of a jerk!)*

NS: On a personal level it was one of the most surprising – and rewarding – aspects of the Rewatch. Joyce was always someone who grated on me, and Joss shaped her to do so, especially for any younger viewer. When I first started watching *Buffy* I was in my early twenties and just coming out of university, and starting my career. So I identified with the younger characters of the shows over the older ones. There are still episodes where Joyce grates on me (see 'Gingerbread') but now that I have young children, I look at them every day and hope I never disappoint them or do the wrong thing and make them hate me. And then, with a sinking feeling, I know that of *course* I will do all those things. Joyce tries to do right by Buffy, but she's just been dumped by a sleazy husband and her daughter is a known troublemaker who forced Joyce to leave her friends behind so she could escape to a place where people didn't know her daughter just burned down the school's gym. Her daughter lies to her on a daily basis, and Joyce still tries to reason with her and make her happy. The scene of her attempting to celebrate Buffy's birthday with the little cupcake still makes me cry.

I'm a big Riley hater, too, and when he was first introduced I thought with some surprise that he might end up changing for me, too. And then … nope, still hate him.

Giles is someone who I've always loved as a character, but again, I watched him differently this time for the same reason that Joyce felt different: I saw him as a parent, struggling to do the right thing for Buffy. Things that before had been sad were now devastating, like the way he protects her like a daughter in 'Helpless' and she turns on him because it's too late. I used to think him singing 'Behind Blue Eyes' in the cafe was hilarious, but now it was bittersweet, because you realize he's in real pain in that scene, and the Scoobies simply don't understand him. He's a middle-aged man who hangs out with high schoolers all the time. That's *got* to be tough.

And Xander's always been a bit of a jerk. That's why I love the guy so much. He wears his heart on his sleeve, and while sometimes that means you just want to *smack him so hard* other times I have to admit that I was thinking the same thing, but he just had the guts to say it. That yellow crayon speech gets me every time …

JKS: *Two of the most fun recaps were group sourced. The first was the 'Beer Bad' war, where contributors to the recap battled over whether the episode was sheer genius, or total crap. [Ed. Note: Bring this episode up to any Whedonian and there is sure to be a lengthy diatribe.] The other was the recap for the musical episode 'Once More With Feeling'. Can you describe how you thought of such creative recaps? (And will you share the lyrics to your 'OMWF' 'Previously on Buffy' song??? Please! Please! Please!)*

NS: It just seemed natural to me that certain episodes require more than just one or two perspectives. I've seen 'Beer Bad' and 'OMWF' so many times and have discussed them for so many years that I knew I could have fun with these weeks. 'Beer Bad' is that episode that was so universally reviled when it first aired that, surprisingly, there was very little online fighting about it: fans simply agreed it was terrible. *TERRIBLE.* (Ed. Note: It's awesome. – JKS] But over time, because its awfulness just became a given, it started to become the cool thing to like it, to come up with ways of defending it. And then the challenge became not only to try to defend it, but to *mean* it when you defended it. I've had people say, 'But I like "Beer Bad"!' to me a lot, and I thought, you know what? I bet in the 28 or so contributors, I could find enough people who actually want to defend it that I could set up a battle royale. And it was SO much fun. The haters hated with so much hate it was hilarious, and the defenders were so passionate they almost convinced me they were right. (Okay, not really; nothing could sway me on that episode.)

As for 'Once More With Feeling', we all know that everyone has a hidden talent somewhere. And the people reading the *Buffy* Rewatch began to familiarize themselves with the contributors to the point where they felt like they knew them week after week. And so, why not show them the hidden talents of these brilliant people? And what better week than 'OMWF', the week where we discovered just how multitalented the *Buffy* cast was? (Okay, also, I wanted to show the academics being total wonderful goofballs.) And they stepped up to the plate with gusto. There was singing, and dancing, and poetry, and parody, and even a talking cup (you have to see it to understand). It took a long time to put it together (I probably spent fifteen hours on that one post) and to organize everyone, but when these people began putting their heads together they came up with routines that were so ingenious I think our recap is almost as entertaining as the episode itself.

While 'OMWF' happened so close to the end of the Rewatch, I still managed to get many of the contributors to do something special for 'Chosen'. You simply can't end a project as huge as this one turned out to be without celebrating the end of it, and talking about that final episode and everything it meant. The final post was scheduled for Tuesday, 27 December (we always did the Rewatch on Tuesdays to mimic *Buffy*'s original broadcast night), and then beginning at 8 a.m. the following morning and continuing until 10 p.m. that night, I posted something from fifteen more contributors every hour, talking about the end, the entire series, or the Rewatch itself. I even got two of our most avid and faithful readers to contribute so their ideas would be front and centre on the blog, and not just in the comments section. It was a wonderful way to end the Rewatch, and to show off so many of our writers at the end. And yes you can reprint my lyrics: I'm flattered you would ask!

(to the tune of 'Going Through the Motions')

Every single week, we all watch *Buffy*
Old viewers and new alike
Then we come on here, and talk about it
All at eight o'clock, every Tuesday night.

'Welcome to the Hellmouth'

'Harvest,' 'Witch,'
No, I won't name them all,
But these three jumpstarted the Rewatch
Back in season one,
I knew back then that this would be big … FUN!

Season two was next, and oh so painful,
Angelus was back and mean,
Buffy took a sword and stuck him with it,
And I cried and cried all throughout the scene.

With Angel gone to Hell
Poor Buffy fell
Into a great big funk
And then we met Eliza Dushku
And her 'dad' the Mayor
Who didn't stand a chance against our Slayer.

Angel left and we got Riley
The Initiative weren't very wily
Season five was not so smiley
'The Gift' and 'The Body' …

But Buffy's come back now
So we'll kick it up a notch
Come along with me
In this very lively
Week of the Buffy
Rewaaaaaatch!

GO FURTHER

Extracts/Essays/Articles
'The Great Buffy Rewatch of 2011 Archive'
Nikki Stafford
Nik at Nite. 29 December 2011, http://nikkistafford.blogspot.com/2011/03/great-buffy-rewatch-archive.html.

Websites
Nik at Nite, http://nikkistafford.blogspot.com/

Chapter
4

*Buffy*speak:
The Internal and External
Impact of Slayer Slang

Liz Medendorp

→ **Apparently Buffy has decided the problem with the English language is all those pesky words.**
  – Xander, 'Bad Eggs' (Season 2, Episode 24), *BtVS*

Fig.1: Disgusted by Buffy's
questions about a dead guy
found stuffed in a locker,
Cordelia replies with,
'Morbid, much?'

The way we speak says a lot about who we are. Accents, dialects, the use of slang, and other verbal cues are strong indicators of our background, and people tend to adopt the speech patterns of those close to them. In this way, groups often distinguish themselves through their particular shared way of speaking. As the above quote from Xander demonstrates, language is something that is consciously played with in the television series *Buffy the Vampire Slayer* and Buffy's way of speaking is explicitly identified as out of the ordinary. Throughout the series, Buffy and her friends, a group referred to as the 'Scooby Gang', consistently use language in a creative and unique way, effectively doing away with 'all those pesky words' and inventing their own form of language that is much more expressive and relevant to their teenage context: *Buffy*speak.

*Buffy*speak is a term that refers to the very distinctive way of speaking used by some of the main characters in the *Buffy*verse, encompassing both the show itself and its spin-off series *Angel*, which may be considered part of the *Buffy* canon, as well as the non-canonical productions of the *Buffy* fan community, including message board postings and fanfiction. *Buffy*speak both draws on *and* influences the conventions of standard American slang, and in some instances, British, and acts as a prime example of language's ability to form group identities and structure communities, both within the show and in the real world.

The style of *Buffyspeak*
The distinctiveness of *Buffy*speak is established very early on in the series. In the very first episode, for example, both Buffy and Xander use the phrase 'What's the sitch?', Buffy says that the library gives her the 'wiggins', and Cordelia reacts to Buffy's enquiries about a dead guy stuffed in a locker with 'Morbid, much?' All of these are classic *Buffy*isms and immediately set the tone for the unique linguistic style of the series. It's hard to pinpoint what exactly characterizes *Buffy*speak, although various elements are identifiable, as evidenced by several in-depth studies of the show's dialogue.

In *Slayer Slang: A 'Buffy the Vampire Slayer' Lexicon* (2003), author Michael Adams addresses the phenomenon of *Buffy*speak as a whole, which includes slayer slang as well as slayer jargon and slayer style. An extensive glossary of *Buffy*isms from both the show (the 'canonical' source) and several online communities dedicated to the *Buffy*verse ('non-canonical' sources) are included in the text. Adams also discusses at length the importance of studying 'ephemeral language'– language patterns that more or less constitute a 'fad' and will soon pass, yet still act as a strong force in the structuring of com-

*Buffy*speak: The Internal and External Impact of Slayer Slang
Liz Medendorp

munities and the verbal atmosphere of the time.

Linguist Jesse Saba Kirchner has also done an in-depth study in this area and developed a computer program that could produce phrases in *Buffy*speak. In order to construct this program, Kirchner had to first establish various levels of *Buffy*isms and determined there are seven different categories: jargon and new vocabulary, affixation, changing parts of speech, syntactic changes, truncation, semantic shift and popular culture references. The importance of this study, however, lies not in the specifics of these different levels, but in demonstrating that slayer slang *does* have defined rules. However, he also determined that the consistent production of effective and novel *Buffy*isms does also require some degree of human creativity.

The distinguishing characteristics of *Buffy*speak can be divided into two major categories: grammatical and lexical. These two categories combine to create the distinctive *stylistic* quality of *Buffy*speak. Grammatical traits such as the addition of prefixes and suffixes, the shifting of parts of speech, and the compounding and shortening of words are extremely common throughout the show, as are lexical elements including a heavy influence of 'valley girl' sayings, the creation of new jargon, and the use of pop culture references. These characteristic stylistic traits are among the primary qualities attributable to the *Buffy*speak phenomenon, and therefore each requires at least a brief review.

Fig.2: Joss Whedon on set surrounded by some über-vamps during the filming of the final episode, 'Chosen' (© 2003 AP / Damian Dovarganes)

Grammatical traits
The members of the Scooby Gang are notorious for adding prefixes and suffixes to their words, and by doing so they shift words from one part of speech to another. For example, when Xander adds *-y* to the end of the verb 'avoid' in the Season 6 episode 'Bargaining, Part 2' (Episode 2), he turns it into an adjective: 'avoidy'. This is arguably the most distinctive and prevalent characteristic of *Buffy*speak. The prefixes and suffixes used by the Scooby Gang are also in common usage in Standard English, which is necessary in order for such affixes to be understood by the audience, yet the uniqueness of the affixes in *Buffy*speak arises from the choice of words to which they attach them. Other notable canonical examples include:

The prefix *un-*, as in 'I'm not *un*worried' (Willow, 'After Life' [Season 6, Episode 3])
The prefix *über-*, as in 'It's the *über*-suck'! (Buffy, 'Inca Mummy Girl' [Season 2, Episode 4]), '*über*-vamps' to refer to the extra-strong Turok-Han breed of vampires, and '*über*-Buffy' ('Primeval' [Season 4, Episode 21])
The suffix *-age*, as in 'Willow kiss*age*' (Oz, 'Innocence' [Season 2, Episode 14])
The suffix *-y*, as in Buffy's response to Giles saying 'Punishing yourself like this is pointless'. 'It's entirely point*y*'! (Buffy, 'When She Was Bad' [Season 2, Episode 1])
The suffix *-ish*, as in 'I'll go... slip into something a little more break-and-enter*ish*' (Buffy,

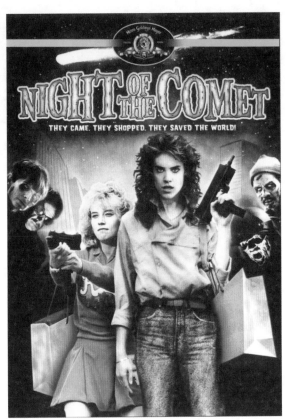

Fig.3: Poster for the 1984
cult horror/sci-fi film 'Night
of the Comet' about two
Valley Girls surviving in a
post-apocalyptic world, a big
influence on Joss Whedon's
conception of Buffy
(© 1984 Thomas Coleman
and Michael Rosenblatt
Productions)

'Enemies' [Season 3, Episode 17])

This last example also demonstrates the Scoobies'
tendency to use long compounds. Often times these
compounds stem from well-known phrases or pop culture references and they very often get a suffix added
to them, especially -y. There are very many examples
of this practice all throughout the series, including
'out-of-the-loopy' ('A New Man' [Season 4, Episode
12]) and 'stiff upper-lippy' ('Bargaining 2' [Season 6,
Episode 2]). Other examples that use this technique
but also incorporate pop culture references include
'heart-of-darknessy' to mean 'depressing' ('Restless'
[Season 4, Episode 22) and 'twelve-steppy', referring
to the twelve-step plan in Alcoholics Anonymous ('Enemies' Season 3, Episode 17]).

Yet the Scoobies don't just combine phrases and
affixes to make long compound words, they also habitually shorten phrases, usually clipping prepositions off
the end of common expressions. Just a few examples
include: deal (with), hanging (out with), wig (out), freak
(out) and messed (up). By shortening these phrases
into recognizable but truncated versions, the Scooby
Gang effectively expresses the same ideas without bogging down their speech with un-
needed extra words, instead finding the most effective way to express an idea.

Lexical traits
The vocabulary of *Buffy*speak is not quite so easy to pin down, as it is constantly expanding even today through the non-canonical *Buffy*speakers of online communities
and fandom. There are, however, strong roots in Valley Girl expressions and some slayer
jargon has been established by both the show itself and the early years of *Buffy*dom
online. The aspect of vocabulary that depends on constant evolution, however, lies in
the persistent and creative use of pop culture references.

The use of the words 'like', 'way', 'totally', 'duh', 'much', and other sayings classically
attributed to the Valley Girl stereotype abound in the *Buffy*verse. Buffy's background as
a cheerleader from LA combined with some of Whedon's sources of inspiration such as,
as Jennifer K. Stuller has noted, the 1984 film *Night of the Comet* (Thom E. Eberhardt),
may explain this heavy influence, although this facet is often overlooked by scholars
of *Buffy*speak. Not wanting to reduce Buffy to a vapid, ditzy girl with poor language
skills, the creative side of her speech is normally the focus, yet it is this mixture of girly

*Buffy*speak: The Internal and External Impact of Slayer Slang
Liz Medendorp

expressions with her clever witticisms and heroism that characterizes Buffy's allure as a protagonist. While it is true that she becomes more serious as the show progresses, it is her persistent lightheartedness and girliness, constantly foregrounded by her Valley Girl speech, that makes Buffy such an interesting, unique and effective heroine.

There also exists plenty of *Buffy* jargon that stems from both the show itself and online communities. Particular terms become characteristic of the slayer trade, such as 'dusting' to refer to staking a vampire, and jargon also exists to refer to components of the show itself, like the 'Scooby Gang', or elements of slayer mythology such as 'Chosen One' or 'Watcher', both key figures in the lore of the series. From the non-canonical sources, members of the online community 'The Bronze' were known as 'Bronzers', and these Bronzers and other members of online *Buffy* fandom use terms specific to their community, such as 'poofage', meaning an abrupt departure, exit or disappearance from the boards, and 'whuppage', meaning work or other responsibilities that keep you from the message boards.

Another key feature of *Buffy*speak is pervasive use of pop culture references. This is already a common teenage phenomenon, but has arguably become increasingly prevalent in the past couple of decades, as can be seen through the popularity of shows like *The Simpsons* (Matt Groening, 1989-), *Family Guy* (Seth MacFarlane, 1999-2002: 2005-)and *South Park* (Trey Parker and Matt Stone, 1997-), all of which heavily utilize pop culture references in their comedy. In *Buffy*, however, then-contemporary trends in popular culture are not merely referenced, but morphed into new terms and expressions that creatively express complex ideas in concise and humorous ways. This unique and effective aspect of *Buffy*speak, along with but probably more so than the use of Valley Girl expressions and specific *Buffy* jargon, has overwhelmingly been adopted and expanded by fans.

One of the most notable methods of doing this involves using names of familiar pop culture figures as verbs. In the Season 1 episode 'The Pack' (Episode 6), Giles expresses his belief that the strange change in Xander's behaviour is merely a result of his being a teenaged boy as opposed to the influence of supernatural forces. Buffy responds: 'I cannot believe you of all people are trying to Scully me!' Anyone familiar with the highly popular television series *The X-Files* (Chris Carter, 1993-2002) would immediately understand the meaning of Buffy's statement, accusing Giles of being overly skeptical. In the episode 'I Only Have Eyes for You' (Season 2, Episode 19), after having been stopped by Buffy from being violent with his girlfriend, a confused boy asks what happened, to which Buffy responds, 'You just went O. J. on your girlfriend!' – a clear reference to the highly publicized O. J. Simpson trial, and a way of using a shared cultural reference to convey a larger point.

Xander also adopts pop culture references into his vocabulary, altering them just enough to express a new idea. Several times he references the word 'lollapalooza', which is the name of an annual music festival, and is also defined by the *Historical Dictionary of Slang* as 'something that is an extraordinary example of its kind'. In the episode 'Halloween' (Season 2, Episode 6), in response to the revelation that Halloween is normally a quiet time of year for fighting the supernatural forces of evil is: 'Halloween, quiet? I figured it would have been a big ole vamp Scareapalooza'. He also uses this construction in the episode 'The Wish' (Season 3, Episode 9), in which he states, 'Look, you wanna do Guiltapalooza, fine, but I'm done with that'. While these expressions are already packed with meaning, the familiar references add an additional level of comprehension.

So where does this distinctive style come from? Since there are rules to the construction, use and style of *Buffy*speak, there must be some level of consistency throughout the *Buffy*verse, both within the canon and without. Obviously the show's team of writers constructed a particular way of speaking for the Scooby Gang, yet with seven seasons of material and two dozen different writers, what is it that created *Buffy*speak and defined its unique qualities which so many fans take joy in replicating? Jane Espenson, who worked on *Buffy* for five of its seven seasons, explains in her introduction to Adams's *Slayer Slang* (2003) that it all begins with Joss Whedon, the visionary creator of the show, and that the writers were 'all doing [their] darndest to do a Joss Whedon impersonation. This is what gives *Buffy* its consistent sound'. The linguistic style of the show comes from Whedon's own speech style; he habitually shortens words ('What's the sitch'? – an expression he has apparently used since college), extends metaphors ('It's not pointless, it's extremely pointy'!), and uses prefixes and suffixes creatively ('not unworried'). In a sense, *Buffy*'s writers were the first 'fans' to appropriate this speech form and add to it. In sum, Whedonspeak is the father of *Buffy*speak, using a combination of its distinctive grammatical and lexical traits to create its unique style. But children all grow up, so *Buffy*speak has since grown through other writers and fans who have contributed more and more to the phenomenon.

The function of *Buffy*speak
Language acts as a crucial element in *Buffy*, especially as a group-building force, and *Buffy*speak is a language used primarily and almost exclusively by the Scooby Gang. In addition, much of the style comes originally from Buffy herself (via Whedon), and her linguistic prowess can be especially seen through her use of witticisms in combat. Yet as *Buffy*speak is adopted by the other Scoobies, they contribute new phrases and expressions that follow established rules. This process works to strengthen and solidify the bond between Buffy and her friends, and the closeness of the group is undeniable throughout the series, partly due to the language style. This process of enhancing group solidarity through the use of a similar language style can also be seen within the fan community, functioning in the same way.

The chapter entitled 'Staking in Tongues', found in Wilcox and Lavery's 2002 *Fighting the Forces*, offers an excellent study of Buffy's use of *Buffy*speak as a weapon – in particular, her trademark use of puns. *Buffy*speak functions as a weapon in combat, so

Buffyspeak: The Internal and External Impact of Slayer Slang
Liz Medendorp

much so, the Scoobies attempt to adopt this tactic as well – thought they lack Buffy's preternatural flair for it. Buffy uses this method of attack against the Master in 'Prophecy Girl' (Season 1, Episode 12), to which he snidely remarks, 'Oh good – the feeble banter portion of the fight'. Then in the third season premiere 'Anne', Willow, also attempts to use language as a weapon, as she so often observed Buffy doing: 'That's right, big boy. Come and get it'. Her awkward attempt at verbal bravado falls flat in comparison to Buffy's usual cleverness and wit in battle. Defending herself to Xander after the fact, Willow says, 'Well, the Slayer always says a pun or a witty play on words and I think it throws the vampires off and makes them frightened that I'm wisecracking and okay, I didn't really have time to work on that one but you try it every time!' In response, Xander admits, 'I've always been amazed with how Buffy fought, but in a way I feel like we took her punning for granted'.

Fig.4: 'The Bronze' nightclub in Sunnydale, the inspiration for the name of the WB-sponsored online Buffy fan forum. Image appeared on 'Buzzmakers: The Blog' article '22 Teen TV After School Hangouts' by user amypiehoneybunch on Sep. 1, 2011.

This scene clearly shows Buffy's status as the original source and most effective user of *Buffy*speak, but it also demonstrates the other Scoobies' attempt to adopt this speaking style. Over time, the other Scoobies learn to wield this slangish weapon as well, although not always in the context of combat, and some more effectively than others. Some individuals, such as Oz and even Anya, use their ability to adopt *Buffy*speak to enter into the group, while others who speak differently, such as Faith, are incapable of ever successfully becoming a full-fledged member of the Scooby Gang. As Adams mentions in his discussion of Slayer Style, 'If, night after night, you slay vampires, you need to know who your friends are, and you know who they are because they speak the same language'. But this method of using language to form group solidarity is used not only by the Scooby Gang within the show, but also by *Buffy* fans all around the world.

The impact of *Buffy*speak
Even though the season finale of *Buffy the Vampire Slayer* is now a decade past, *Buffy*speak continues to live on. As Jane Espenson noted, it may have begun with Joss Whedon's idiosyncratic speech patterns, but this has been expanded and perpetuated by the fan community. Message boards and fanfiction are two particularly active areas where the production of *Buffy*speak continues to be used and expanded. Through message boards, fanfiction and online communities, fans have adopted the speech patterns of the Scooby Gang as a means of unifying the vast community of *Buffy* fans. In this way, the unique group identity of the Scooby Gang has been translated into a much broader, yet just as strong, unified community of fans.

Just as in the *Buffy* series, *Buffy*speak has been a defining factor for constructing communities both online and in real life. Adams goes into depth about two online communities in particular, 'The Bronze' and 'The Bronze: Beta'. These two forums offer(ed) a place for *Buffy* fans to come together and discuss any and all aspects of *Buffy*dom, so it is not surprising that members of these online communities very quickly adopted *Buffy*speak into their speech patterns. Not only did the use of *Buffy*isms help form a specific group identity due to the conscious verbal affiliation with the show, but it also strengthened the *Buffy*speak phenomenon itself, expanding its use and encouraging further non-canonical additions to the *Buffy* lexicon.

Buffy fans have adopted the rules of *Buffy*speak into their own speech patterns, including suffixing, compounding and pop culture references. In fact, many of the entries in Adams's glossary come from these boards as opposed to being produced by the show writers themselves. The use of suffixes, in particular, reaches every corner of the *Buffy*verse, and the vast majority of Adams's examples of *-age* suffixing were actually produced by Bronzers and Beta-ers. Terms specific to these message boards include 'postage', 'lurkage', 'whuppage' and 'poofage'. Even the academic community surrounding *Buffy* studies uses this practice, with both a quarterly journal and a biennial conference adopting the title 'Slayage'.

The *Buffy*verse also acts as a popular basis for fanfiction, and thus *Buffy*speak has a strong presence there as well. But *Buffy*speak not only characterizes *Buffy* fanfiction, as it has also been used into otherwise unrelated sub-cultures of fanfiction, including *Stargate* (Roland Emmerich, 1994), *Harry Potter* (J.K. Rowling, 1997 - 2007) and *The West Wing* (Aaron Sorkin, 1999-2006), to name a few. All of these fanverses seem to have been influenced by *Buffy*speak, especially through the adoption of its particular grammatical traits such as suffixing and shifting parts of speech. It is impossible to definitively say that this was a conscious influence, and in fact it probably was more of an involuntary seepage of *Buffy*speak into the linguistic style of the larger community of fanfiction writers. But the fact that this transfer was likely more or less involuntary actually demonstrates the great power and impact of *Buffy*speak on non-canonical fan productions as a structuring force for communities.

Even on the popular site *reddit.com*, a subcommunity exists dedicated solely to *Buffy*, and although it is one of the smaller subreddits, at the time of this writing it still connects nearly 5,000 *Buffy*fans in an online forum format. This subreddit also has a reasonably active membership, as it is very rare that any post goes unnoticed or undiscussed. Prompted by a discussion of favourite *Buffy*isms, the 'potentials', as they call themselves, affirmed that they do in fact use phrases akin to 'morbid, much?', 'love makes you do the wacky' and 'vague that up for me'. There was also a high response with regard to the use of specific jargon produced by *Buffy*, such as 'wiggins', 'Big Bad' and 'bitca', which can immediately identify the speaker as a *Buffy*fan. The use of pop culture references has also come into common usage even in these fans' daily lives.

Overall, it seems clear that the online *Buffy* fan community, whether on a message board, a fanfiction site or *reddit*, has wholeheartedly welcomed the use of *Buffy*speak among its members, encouraging a continued spirit of creativity and production of new *Buffy*isms, as well as a perpetuation of established, canonical ones. This gives *Buffy* fan-

*Buffy*speak: The Internal and External Impact of Slayer Slang
Liz Medendorp

dom as a whole a sense of unification, bringing fans together not only to speak and discuss, but to communicate in what is essentially a unique language, solidifying a sense of group identity of *Buffy*fans who use *Buffy*speak in both their online fan communities and in their day-to-day life. ●

GO FURTHER

Books

Why Buffy Matters: The Art of Buffy the Vampire Slayer
Rhonda Wilcox
(London: I.B. Tauris, 2005)

Slayer Slang: A 'Buffy the Vampire Slayer' Lexicon
Michael Adams
(New York: Oxford University Press, 2003)

Historical Dictionary of American Slang
Ed. J.E. Lighter
(New York: Random House, 1997)

Extracts/Essays/Articles

'I Can't Believe I'm Saying It Twice in the Same Century ... but "Duh ..".: The Evolution of *Buffy the Vampire Slayer* Sub-Culture Language through the Medium of Fanfiction'
Katrina Blasingame
In *Slayage: The Online International Journal of Buffy Studies*. 5: 4 (2006),
http://slayageonline.com/PDF/Blasingame.pdf.

'And in Some Language That's English? Slayer Slang and Artificial Computer Generation'
Jesse Saba Kirchner
In *Slayage: The Online International Journal of Buffy Studies*. 5: 4 (2006),
http://slayageonline.com/PDF/Kirchner.pdf.

'Getting a Wiggins and Being a Bitca: How Two Items of Slayer Slang Survive on *Television Without Pity* Message Boards'
Mark Peters
In *Slayage: The Online International Journal of Buffy Studies*. 5: 4 (2006), http://slayageonline.com/PDF/Peters.pdf.

'Introduction'
Jane Espenson
In Michael Adams. *Slayer Slang: A 'Buffy the Vampire Slayer' Lexicon* (New York: Oxford University Press, 2003), pp. vii–xii.

'Staking in Tongues: Speech Act as Weapon in *Buffy*'
Karen Eileen Overbey and Preston-Matto Lahney
In Rhonda V. Wilcox and David Lavery (eds). *Fighting the Forces: What's at Stake in Buffy the Vampire Slayer* (Lanham, MD: Rowman & Littlefield Publishers, Inc., 2002), pp. 73–84.

Chapter
5

'Welcome to The Hellmouth': Harnessing the Power of Fandom in the Classroom

Amy Peloff and David Boarder Giles

→ INTRODUCTION: WE'RE ALL SCOOBIES

Most academics do what they do – research, write, teach – with regard to the things they are most passionate about. Sometimes it's feminism. Sometimes it's technology. Sometimes it's literary theory. And sometimes it's *Buffy the Vampire Slayer*. Except, in the latter case, what they 'do' isn't actually *Buffy*, it's feminism, or technology, or literary theory, or … you get the idea.

Fig.1: The passion of acafandom can sometimes be analogous to the mobs of murderously lovelorn Sunnydale women under Xander's botched love spell in 'Bewitched, Bothered, and Bewildered'. ['Bewitched, Bothered and Bewildered,' Marti Noxon, James A. Contner, 1998, Mutant Enemy, Inc.]

Buffy (and other popular media) provide Doublemeat Palace - worthy material through which to productively explore complex ideas and theories. It's also fun – not just for the teacher who gets to share her passion for her chosen field, but also for her students who can connect their passion for *Buffy* with the course content. Most importantly, teachers' and students' mutual fandom represents a shared knowledge base upon which to build a learning community. This connection fosters a sense of trust based on a recognition of shared identity that underpins student and teacher growth alike: we're all Scoobies.

Buffy's power has been unleashed in the classroom and the academy virtually since the show's first episode in 1997. The first issue of *Slayage: The Online International Journal of Buffy Studies* appeared by 2001. And entire courses are now taught about and through *Buffy* in classrooms and universities all over the world. Fans have made *Buffy* a gateway (or hellmouth) into the university – its communities, its physical spaces, and its languages. Above all, in the classroom, the series both models and facilitates *accessible curricula, collaborative work* and *critical inquiry*. Aided by its characters and writing, fans (students and teachers alike) are cultivating more diverse, more decentralized classrooms, wherein they can explore the complexities of morality, modernity and gender articulated by the programme. And – not insignificantly – they are having fun doing it.

'Aca-fans' are both fans and scholars – lucky folks who are able to combine their passion for something (in this case, *Buffy*) with their scholarly writing, research, and teaching. While the concept of the aca-fan has existed for roughly twenty years, the term still reads uneasily. On one hand, fans can be obsessive (here, picture the mobs of murderously lovelorn **Sunnydale** women under Xander's botched love spell in 'Bewitched, Bothered, and Bewildered' [Season 2, Episode 16]) and loyal to the point of losing their objectivity. On the other hand, while universities certainly encourage scholars to be passionate about their work, they are still held accountable to a mythical, elusive standard of objectivity. To be an aca-fan, then, is to straddle the uncomfortable boundary between participant and observer, detached scientist and squee-emitting enthusiast.

Yet, despite its challenges, the combination of academic pursuits with impassioned fandom has its benefits. If we have learned **one thing** from the eyebrow-raising love between a certain vampire slayer and her vampire lover(s), it's that good things can come from transgressing boundaries. Taking to heart Buffy's refusal to follow a rule made up by 'a bunch of men who died thousands of years ago' (as she puts it in 'Chosen' [Season

'Welcome to the Hellmouth':
Harnessing the Power of Fandom in the Classroom
Amy Peloff and David Boarder Giles

7, Episode 22]), *Buffy* scholars aspire to new frontiers for research, writing, theorizing and teaching.

Accessing the *Buffy*verse:
Accessibility and exclusivity in the classroom

Using *Buffy* as both content and inspiration for peda-gogy within the classroom opens up exciting new pos-sibilities. Not the least of its benefits is that it creates a space into which students can enter as experts – or at least feel competent to participate in discussions about the material. The availability and accessibility of *Buffy* establishes a fairly democratic foundation for a course. Even if they haven't seen it, students can easily find the series through local libraries or Netflix. And because *Buffy* was produced for a network audience, it isn't too violent, too sexual or even too complicated – network censors work to ensure that social norms are not graphically challenged and the economics of maintaining both viewers and advertis-ers inhibits creativity and transgressiveness. A show that wanders too far outside the familiar tropes and styles of mainstream television risks cancellation. Therefore, most viewers can consume most network television series – including one as rich as *Buffy* – easily and without the provocation of the truly unfamiliar. *Buffy* still manages to in-novate, however, by invoking familiar character types and storytelling devices and then subverting them.

Fig.2: The classroom frequently feels like an unsafe space in which public humiliation is a nightmare waiting to spring to life. ['Nightmares,' David Greenwalt and Joss Whedon, Bruce Seth Green, 1997, Mutant Enemy, Inc.]

While network television is committed to providing a formulaic experience for a ge-neric audience, academia has often had very different values. Learning is frequently un-comfortable and intentionally challenging. Sticking to well-worn assumptions and ideas is antithetical to the work of academia. And yet the mind-blowing work that is done within classrooms can have a negative flipside – an elitism and exclusivity that leaves large seg-ments of the population feeling unwelcome. Students who're unfamiliar with the univer-sity's jargon and conduct can feel isolated. Even the most enthusiastic student can feel alienated and humbled. The language of academia – 'post-structuralism', 'feminism', 'se-miotics', 'postcolonialism', 'critical race theory' and so on – combines with some students' ability to casually name-drop Butler, Deleuze, Spivak, Foucault and Said (for example) to create an environment in which some students feel entitled to participate and others feel increasingly marginalized. Unlike television, academia has never been known for its inter-est in providing a welcoming space for broad audiences or ensuring that its ideas can be easily grasped in 50-minute segments. Instead it adheres to a more medieval apprentice system that expects students to devote years of their lives to learning at the feet of their masters. It is not unlike the Watchers Council in these matters.

In contrast, grounding a course within the *Buffy*verse can alleviate some of the feel-ings of 'imposter syndrome' – the feeling that you don't belong in the classroom and that it is simply a matter of time before this fact is publicly and humiliatingly revealed (as when

Xander literally shows up to class wearing only his underwear in 'Nightmares' [Season 1, Episode 10]). While students and instructors alike are afflicted by this syndrome, fans of the show are often *very* confident, even encyclopaedic, about their knowledge. That assurance can empower students to actively participate in a class – and in even larger intellectual projects. (Consider the panel at the biennial 'Slayage' conference for people who have written books about *Buffy*: each year, more people sit on the panel who were in the audience the year before.) The number of *Buffy* fans who self-select into classes with 'Buffy' in the title surely reflects this empowerment. But even for newcomers to the show, mastering – or at least becoming mildly competent in – the *Buffy*verse is significantly less daunting than grasping the whole of postcolonial theory. Watching an episode of *Buffy* is relatively painless, and ultimately, even non-fans can develop a fan-like passion, or at least appreciation, for the show, which can become a pathway into the discussion.

Tackling the 'Big Bad' together: Modelling a collaborative classroom

If *Buffy* makes for more accessible course material and broader classroom participation, the show's content can also open up the ways we think about the structure, pedagogy and students' experience of the course. Especially if students and teachers alike are already fans – already experts, in a way – the work of 'teaching' a course becomes a much more collaborative, decentralized project. Fans genderediolencecisms about intimateigh stakes topics like race or gender in the classroom. n a way that their fan-peers can helpdon't need to rely upon a teacher to make sense of it for them in the same way they might for, say, *Paradise Lost* (John Milton, 1667). And while non-fans in the classroom may have some catching up to do, this is catching up with which their fan-peers can help. *Buffy*-centric pedagogy, then, can help model the value of student-centred teaching and peer-facilitation.

Of course, this is all true of any popular television show. One of the things that make us love *Buffy* so much is also the thing that makes it so perfect for a collaborative classroom: the emphasis on cooperation and communal problem-solving. The show offers tangible, relatable characterizations of a spectrum of participatory behaviours that offer a productive model for a classroom-based learning community. Each character's foibles and strengths ultimately adds up to a team which is more than the sum of its parts: only together can they tackle the 'Big Bad' and save the day.

So the spectrum of well-fleshed out character types on *Buffy* doesn't just make it good television. It multiplies the perspectives from which an audience might identify with, understand, and make use of the show. In the same way that each Scooby is a valued member of the team with unique attributes and skills, students can recognize how a range of voices, backgrounds, life histories and personalities are crucial for dynamic classroom experiences. Exploring this diversity can facilitate more deliberate, collaborative dialogue within the learning community. Having the class identify what kind of Scooby-student they are, for example, can spark a discussion about how and why we participate in class-

'Welcome to the Hellmouth':
Harnessing the Power of Fandom in the Classroom
Amy Peloff and David Boarder Giles

rooms in the ways we do. Once we've acknowledged our patterns, we can work together to bring out the best in each other, and challenge ourselves to move beyond our comfort zones.

Here, again, what makes us love *Buffy* is what makes it more than just an interesting subject for a class. The dedication the show inspires in its fans applies not just to their viewership. They often translate the power and motivation of *Buffy*'s characters, their strengths and struggles, directly into aspiration and resolve in their own personal growth. These qualities are wonderful catalysts for intellectual and interpersonal collaboration, in *and* out of the classroom. Some of our favourite characters illustrate this well.

Fig. 3: In the same way that Xander's unique attributes and skills form a fundamental part of the Scooby ensemble, diverse skills and knowledges are crucial to the functioning of a learning community ['Grave,' David Fury, James A. Contner, 2002, Mutant Enemy, Inc.]

For example, Xander, the perpetual sidekick, feels continually underqualified and peripheral; his lacklustre academic accomplishments compared to the other Scoobies are often highlighted. Because his learning style is not accommodated within traditional educational structures, he is assumed to be less intelligent and less capable than the other students. But his value to the group is consistently upheld. In episode after episode, derogatory remarks are made about his contribution to the team, but the series refutes their implications, as he provides crucial support throughout the show. Of course, Xander has the odd chance to heroically vanquish his reputation as the useless, goofy Scooby: in 'The Zeppo' (Season 3, Episode 13), for example, having been told by Buffy to remain 'fray-adjacent' so he doesn't get hurt (and relegated to the position of donut procurer, no less) he finds himself at the centre of a supernatural crisis and saves the day alone. But, more importantly, the series regularly asserts the value of his character's unique attributes and skills *as fundamental parts of an ensemble* – most powerfully as the 'heart' in Season 4's 'Primeval' (Season 4, Episode 21) and as the only one who can stop Dark Willow from destroying the world in Season 6's 'Grave' (Episode 22). Xander's talents, although less obvious than other Scoobies', are crucial to the group. The value of characters like Xander is inestimable for inspiring confidence and self-worth in fans and newcomers alike with the same sort of self-doubts. This is every bit as valuable in the classroom as it is in the living room.

Moreover, the value of each Scooby is not grounded simply in their strengths, but in the related fact that they are also eminently flawed. These flaws may be equally the basis for a fan's identification with the character and can be equally useful in the classroom. In contrast to Xander, for example, Willow offers us a characterization of a top student, focused on doing things correctly in order to win approval. Willow's lack of self-confidence expresses itself in a strong desire to please, so much of her early education is grounded less in her own passions and more in a desire to be rewarded with attention. Ignored at home, she seeks validation through her identity as a dependably outstanding student who eagerly embraces the role of teacher's pet. Once her need for love and respect has been satisfied, she blossoms into a strong, independent scholar and witch of epic proportions. The damage from her early years of neglect still exert influence over her, even as she matures, leaving her prone to respond selfishly and viciously to perceived attacks on her support system. The flipside to this insecurity is a deep loyalty to her chosen community.

Even our heroine is not immune from a few all-too-human flaws. Buffy's apathetic attitude towards school – a consequence of her predestination as 'the Chosen One' – obscures her impressive intelligence. For example, in 'What's My Line, Part 1' (Season 2, Episode 9) Buffy's sense that her 'future is pretty much a non-issue' informs her alienation from the day-to-day life of high school. Unlike other students, she knows what her future holds, but she has no sense of control over how it will all play out. Her future is decided no matter what she does, so she is disengaged, apathetic and unwilling to participate. She has no reason to try. Her not-entirely-cosy relationship with academics, her intelligence, powerlessness and resistance, make her relatable for almost anyone who has ever attended high school (or worked in retail, had a parking ticket, or had any other frustrating relationship with a large institution, for that matter). Unlike many other strong female characters – say, Xena, Wonder Woman, or Murphy Brown, to take a few examples – this everydayness gives Buffy a particular credibility to fans. Exactly this relatability also makes her a reassuring presence in the classroom, in contrast to the sometimes opaque, intimidating world of the academe.

Despite her ambivalence about both school and her destiny, however, Buffy excels as a slayer. She is more street-smart than book-smart. Her intuition and critical thinking take over where her lacklustre study skills leave off. And while she has yet to learn how to control her own destiny, Buffy is committed to supporting other people in the realization of their aspirations (an invaluable trait in the classroom). Her loyalty, her championing the underdog, her commitment to 'good', and her willingness to sacrifice everything to protect the people she loves, make her the kind of heroine who inspires sincere devotion in fans. And while we can't all be slayers, her moral compass and personal resolve can orient us in more mundane projects – including our classroom endeavours.

It is both fun and instructive to think about how such disparate personalities were forged into a remarkably productive learning community. Having identified individual strengths and weaknesses, the group developed strategies to benefit from the strengths and compensate for the weaknesses. The point is that it actually takes the whole group to be a functional whole – their individual fallibility actually reinforces the need for each other. This diversity of tactics and traits invites a range of fans and students to take inspiration from *Buffy*'s characters. Like the proverbial blind men describing different parts of an elephant to each other ('It's a tree!' 'No, it's a horse!' 'No, it's a python!'), *Buffy* models a more holistic, collaborative kind of knowledge production than many other television shows – and many other classrooms, for that matter.

'Welcome to the Hellmouth':
Harnessing the Power of Fandom in the Classroom
Amy Peloff and David Boarder Giles

Watching the Watchers: Morality, critical inquiry and the canon

In addition to modelling the value of a diverse, dynamic learning community and help-ing facilitate its creation through accessible content, *Buffy* also provides a gateway (or hellmouth, as the case may be) to complex and hard-core academic content. More than many pop-cultural productions, the show's writers deliberately challenge dominant cul-tural narratives and assumptions – not least of all prevailing assumptions about what women can and can't do on television! In other words, *Buffy* is already doing work similar to many academic analysts. And fans are, in a way, already students, because they are al-ready thinking through these complex issues with the characters. Harnessing the power of fandom within the classroom, then, not only makes learning more fun and accessible. It also gives already passionate fans new ways to interact with subjects and material that are familiar and important to them. What's more, students who come to the show through the classroom, rather than the reverse, may develop the same kind of critical appreciation for the show and its implicit critical analysis. (In this sense, teaching with *Buffy* is a way of expanding the ranks of its fans – even if students don't always call them-selves 'fans' once the course is over!)

As other *Buffy* scholars have illustrated, the show offers a rich text for exploring lan-guage, morality, philosophy, identity politics, psychoanalysis, post-structuralism and so on. The fact that Joss Whedon conceived the show to destabilize our assumptions about what it means to be young, blonde, female and attractive in a story about monsters of-fers signposts for rethinking many of the categories that govern our social worlds. When Buffy walks into the dark alley alone searching for somewhere to hide from whatever is following her in the very first episode, we can't help but anticipate the worst. Yet she defies our pre-programmed expectations by getting the drop on Angel as he makes a typically awkward attempt to introduce himself to her.

While Angel's story prompts meditations about the question of human nature, these are anchored to religious notions of the soul. In contrast, Spike's storyline upsets the show's reliance on such Christian-centric metaphysics and affords opportunities to re-think our assumptions about the clear lines between good and evil: he falls in love despite his soullessness, aligns with the Scoobies after his *Clockwork Orange*-like pacification, and embraces his viciousness despite recovering his soul. From his earliest introduction, Spike's nuances throw Angel's archetypal simplicity into relief. Spike's hopelessly roman-tic nature, for example, persists even after becoming 'sired'. His first independent act as a vampire (in 'Lies My Parents Told Me' [Season 7, Episode 17]) is that of a devoted son. De-termined to share his new, eternal life with his tuberculosis-afflicted mother, he turns her. The questions raised by these incongruous human emotions are piqued by her personality shift once she rises from the dead: her vitriolic rejection of him crushes Spike and illumi-nates the character's on-going emotional vulnerability – despite the apparent loss of his soul to the dark. What is emotion, or the self, we are left to ask, if not anchored in a soul? Spike kills her because the demon he 'set loose' was not the same woman who loved him.

In addition, the inconsistencies between Spike's nature and the canonical knowledge about vampires collected by the Watchers Council over the years reflect not a laziness on the part of the series' writers, but rather a more interesting consideration of the reliability of historical sources. *Buffy* reminds us to reflect on who wrote the histories we read, what inspired them, and how those things impact the stories they wrote down. This emphasis on critical inquiry may be one thing which attracts fans in the first place (or makes fans out of students in the classroom). As Buffy discovers again and again, the Watchers Council is neither benign nor selfless. Not only its policies, but its very foundations, demand scrutiny. In 'Checkpoint' (Season 5, Episode 12) Buffy finally realizes the council's existence depends upon hers: 'You're Watchers. Without a Slayer, you're pretty much just watchin' *Masterpiece Theater*'. Moreover, the knowledge they share with her is not simply limited by their transparency, but also by their capacity to understand it themselves. What Buffy herself realizes – and what the entire series reiterates – is that our very survival is predicated on our willingness to question canonical knowledge. This imperative to challenge does not preclude a respect for the work of the past, but rather urges an active engagement with it, an intellectual sparring match in which weaknesses are identified, strengths are augmented, and new possibilities are illuminated collaboratively. Fans take precisely this call for critical engagement seriously in many aspects of their lives. When they bring it with them to the classroom, it often opens up onto broader critical engagements – the feminism, post-structuralism, critical race theory, postcolonialism and the other bodies of cultural theory described earlier, for example.

Conclusion

Inviting *Buffy* fandom into the classroom violates the mythical ideal that academia engages with 'serious' texts from an objective, location-less standpoint. But, similar to the unyielding conservatism of the Watchers Council, academia is well served by challenges to its habits of thought and behaviour. Any iteration of popular culture can provide productive material for analysis, despite (and, in some ways, because of) the limitations imposed by a production process that is economically bound not to violate the values and aesthetics that (it assumes) belong to the most hegemonic, generic audience – all too often middle class, white, male, English-speaking Americans. Yet even within this field of potential fodder for analysis, *Buffy* stands out as an especially rich, complex and frankly feminist text. Because *Buffy* does provide such meaty content, courses built around it can accomplish a lot. They encourage students to think critically about their engagement with course material and their participation in the classroom. Whether students and teachers come to the classroom as fully-fledged aca-fans, or they develop a growing appreciation for the show through their classroom exposures, both the show and the educational projects that rest upon it succeed to the extent that they bring together – in both the classroom and the living room – a viewing, thinking, questioning public. ●

'Welcome to the Hellmouth':
Harnessing the Power of Fandom in the Classroom
Amy Peloff and David Boarder Giles

~~~~~~~~~~~~~~~

GO FURTHER

Books

Fan Cultures
Matt Hills
(London: Routledge, 2002)

Buffy in the Classroom: Essays on Teaching with the Vampire Slayer
Jodie A. Kreider and Meghan K. Winchell
(North Carolina: McFarland, 2010)

I CAN KILL
A COUPLE OF GEEKS
ALL BY MYSELF.
BUT, HEY,
IF YOU'D LIKE TO
WATCH...
I MEAN, THAT'S WHAT
YOU WATCHERS ARE
GOOD AT, RIGHT?
WATCHING?

WILLOW
SEASON SIX

Fan Appreciation no.2
Rhonda Wilcox, the 'Mother' of *Buffy* Studies

Photo by Richard Gess

Rhonda Wilcox, the 'Mother of *Buffy* Studies', is a professor of English at Gordon State College in Barnesville, GA and the editor, co-editor and author of several books including, *Why Buffy Matters: The Art of Buffy the Vampire Slayer* (I.B. Tauris, 2005) and *Fighting the Forces: What's at Stake in Buffy the Vampire Slayer* (Rowman and Littlefield, 2002), co-edited with the 'Father of *Buffy* Studies', David Lavery. Along with Lavery, she is the founding editor of *Slayage: The Journal of the Whedon Studies Association.*

Jennifer K. Stuller (JKS): *How did you discover* Buffy the Vampire Slayer *and when did you become a fan?*

Rhonda Wilcox (RW): I remember thinking that the name of the series meant either that it would be very, very bad or very, very good – and I became a fan during the first episode. I do admit, though, that at first I did not expect great art, just great fun. By the end of the first season, though, I was starting to understand how impressive it was.

JKS: *You and David Lavery had both previously done work with pop culture studies prior to the* Buffy *studies Phenomena. How did you two meet, and how did 'Buffy studies' come to be? (Or why you, at that time? Was it a matter of zeitgeist?)*

RW: We got to know each other through PCAS, the Popular Culture Association in the South. Dennis Hall, the former editor of *Studies in Popular Culture*, told me that he thought David was a really good editor when David was putting together the *X-Files* book he did with Jill Hague and Marla Cartwright, and to which I contributed (I wrote an essay with J. P. Williams, who had published an important piece on *Moonlighting*, on which I'd published a little piece). Later, when David was thinking of doing a book on *Buffy*, he contacted me because I had published one of the first academic articles on it. J. P. and I had been talking about it by phone as the series aired, and I kept saying I wasn't going to write on it, and she kept saying, 'Oh, yes you will'. She could tell by the way I talked about it. I think there are quite a number of us who write about television as (in SOME ways) a branch of literature, and that is in part because television had, I think, gotten better and better. Of course you can analyse *Buffy* from many different angles, but that is, I think, part of the zeitgeist element you suggest – the creators of TV were getting more and more impressive, and a bunch of us opened our eyes enough to see that.

JKS: *Do you see* Buffy *studies in and of itself as an act of fan phenomena? How, in your experience, is Whedonverse studies different from other studies of popular culture?*

RW: Like *Buffy* itself, it is a both/and sort-of-yes-sort-of-no phenomenon; just as *Buffy* mixes genres, *Buffy* studies crosses categories. It is both scholarship and admiration. I am a Whedon fan just as I am a Dickens fan. (I need to get together the money someday to go to one of the Dickens conferences.) I will note this: if Dickens were alive, it would be really exciting to watch his career unfold. People did, in fact, react in a fannish way to Dickens (read about his performance/reading tours of America sometime) – though there were also contemporary critics who denigrated his work. It's not that different for Whedon.

JKS: *At the time of this interview, the* Slayage Conference on the Whedonverses *just convened for its fifth biennial conference. How did the journal, conference, and the Whedon Studies Association form?*

RW: Oh, my. Well, when David and I were putting together *Fighting the Forces*, there were far more good proposals for chapters than we could fit in the book, so he (inspired by the *Xena* online *Whoosh*) suggested that we start doing the journal. (I will note that it was the idea of my husband, Richard Gess, to call it *Slayage*.) As for the conference, after the East Anglia conference in 2002, David asked MTSU to host a conference in Nashville in 2004, but they didn't want to do another one, so we did the next one, the 2006 conference, here in Georgia at Gordon College, and it kept going from there. As for the WSA, we thought that we in effect were an organization already, so we wanted to make it official. Tanya R. Cochran, David and I found out that making it official can take many hours of labour; it is not hard to become an organization, but becoming an IRS-approved 501 (c) (3) is extremely complex. Tanya in particular put in many hours, and I went through some interesting experiences in downtown Atlanta myself, talking face-to-face with people who kindly tried to tell me things without officially telling me things. Anyway, it was all worth it, because the people who study Whedon are really – I am having a hard time finding the right way to put this: I think they are intellectually and morally good people, and I think that is because they are responding to intellectually and morally good work.

JKS: *You recently received 'Class Protector' umbrellas signed by confer-*

ence attendees and a plaque recognizing your outstanding leadership in Whedon studies including the founding of the Slayage Journal, the Slayage Conference and the Whedon Studies Association. (Tears of pride and appreciation were shed by all.) How does Buffy *in particular reflect and inspire the intellectual, professional and community aspects of Whedon studies?*

RW: Every time I watch 'The Prom' I cry. Now I expect I will cry more. Don't get me started on the umbrella! Oh, my goodness. Okay, as for the actual question: Buffy is not the person I identified with first – that was Willow. But Buffy *tries* even though her 'life happens to, on occasion, suck beyond the telling of it' – and that in the end is why we watch. And it is a joy to be in a room full of people who admire the themes this work invokes.

JKS: *What has been the personal and professional impact of combining your fandom for* Buffy *with academia?*

RW: It is difficult to express; for each of these questions I could have said much more. It has meant many different things. I had long been writing on good television, but *Buffy* gave me a better subject than I had ever had before; it is inspiring material. It has also meant that I travelled to places I never expected to go, because people wanted me to come and lecture on *Buffy*. If you had told me when I was in grad school at Duke that I would be travelling around lecturing on a teenage girl who killed vampires with a stake, I really don't think I would have believed you. Of course, there are a lot of people who didn't believe it; there are always those who scorn our work for a variety of reasons – most of those reasons based in ignorance (in my opinion) – and I'm talking about academics, too. But no one can know every subject. And I do think that more and more people understand that television (even – gasp – fantasy television) can be art – and I think Whedon and his collaborators and *Buffy* in particular have helped to change that.

JKS: *What do you see as the future of Whedon studies in general, and* Buffy *studies in particular? (Especially with the Season 8 and 9 comics and transmedia storytelling.) How might it continue to evolve?*

RW: I think it will continue to grow. Probably, as with most disciplines, there will be an ebb and flow. But the fact that Whedon and his collaborators work in various media is one of the reasons that Whedon studies will grow; this use of multiple platforms is a very modern phenomenon. But it is the heart of the story, not the platform, that will make Whedon studies continue to thrive.

JKS: *How does your personal fandom for* Buffy *influence your work in the classroom/pedagogy? How do students respond to the use of* Buffy *as a teaching tool? Have you seen students connect their fandom to* Buffy *through their studies in inspiring or creative ways?*

RW: This may surprise you, but I have only once taught *Buffy* itself, in an honours class on feminism and fantasy. It was a pleasure to see that once we covered a few episodes, students watched many more, on their own. I've worked with other individual students who wanted to write about *Buffy* for various reasons – one of the main ones being that sense of feeling different, and the wonderful way *Buffy* handles that. I have been spending so much time on organizational stuff for WSA. that I have not had the time to be able to do a proposal for a *Buffy* course; sad, huh?

JKS: *Bonus Question: What are your top five favourite episodes and why?*

RW: 'Restless' – its brilliant allusiveness, wonderful visuals, dreamlike narrative, all the symbols; 'The Body' – the way it conveys pain and loss, perfectly combining the form and the feeling; 'Once More with Feeling' – the joy of the music and the musical, the way it plays with so many narrative threads; 'Surprise / Innocence' – the symbolism, the caring of all the characters; 'Passion' – darkness; or 'Fool for Love' – the amazing editing of past with present; or 'Hush' – so damn scary, so graceful; or – come on, just five?????

~~~~~~~~~~

GO FURTHER

Websites

Slayage: The Journal of the Whedon Studies Association, http://slayageonline.com/

Whoosh, http://whoosh.org/

Chapter 6

Buffy, Dark Romance and Female Horror Fans

Lorna Jowett

→ When asked, in a 2002 *SFX* magazine reader's poll, 'What's the thing you're proudest of in this world?' Joss Whedon, creator of TV show *Buffy the Vampire Slayer*, answered: 'Art and feminism; my little show that changed things'. In February 2012 *The Guardian* newspaper ran an article titled 'Buffy drives home an important issue for women', in which Naomi Alderman suggests that the *Buffy Season* 9 comic series continues to debate significant questions for women (in this case abortion).

Whedon always insisted that the series' premise was an exercise in gender role reversal, and it is now easy to see *Buffy* as a 'little show that changed things' where TV's representation of female, and male, characters is concerned. Characters like Ripley (debuting in the 1979 film *Alien* [Ridley Scott, 1979]) or Sarah Connor (from *The Terminator* [James Cameron, 1984]) may have introduced the female action hero in cinema; *Buffy the Vampire Slayer*, argues Robert Moore, changed the face of television and Emily Nussbaum observed in the *New York Times* in 2002 that 'the show's influence can be felt everywhere'. Specifically *Buffy* can be positioned as a key influence on the contemporary Dark Romance (sometimes called paranormal romance or urban fantasy) publishing and media boom. Just as *Buffy* draws on previous female action heroes from comic books, movies, fiction and TV, Dark Romances from *Twilight* movies (2008-12)to HBO television show *True Blood* (Alan Ball, 2008-) offer variations on *Buffy*'s complex representation of romance, sexuality and gender. Now that VILF (Vampire I'd Like to Fuck) has entered the lexicon, the Dark Romance (in which a female protagonist falls in love with a dark hero, usually a vampire or werewolf, though sometimes another supernatural male) has truly arrived.

Dark Romance isn't necessarily new: the disposable fiction market used to churn out female gothic paperbacks and Dark Romance is just the latest variation. As Lyda Morehouse observes in *Whedonistas!* (2011) 'it would be unfair to say that Joss Whedon single-handedly created' Dark Romance, yet '*Buffy* did a hell of a lot to popularize it'. *Buffy* wasn't just about romance, as explained below, but the subsequent success of the Dark Romances it influences suggests that romance, even as a superficial focus, pushes the right buttons with a female (often heterosexual) audience. So how do these serial fictions appeal directly to women, even to women who might not normally read or watch something categorized as horror?

Firstly, perhaps most obviously, Dark Romances have female protagonists. They may not always be female heroes, but their narratives take a female perspective. This plays out in various ways. In an interview with Joe Nazzaro published in 2002, David Greenwalt, co-executive producer of *Buffy* and co-creator of *Angel the Series* (1999-2004), says that '*Buffy* is about how hard it is to be a woman, and *Angel* is about how hard it is to be a man'. The notion of a narrative focusing on the problems of being a woman is prevalent in all the Dark Romances.

Dark Romance also offers the pleasure of fantasy. One of its fantasies is the ready availability of its desirable protagonists (male and female). *Buffy*, as a US network TV show, was populated by attractive young actors even if some of them were playing geeks and nerds. *Twilight* star Kristen Stewart (Bella) was voted number six of *FHM*'s 100 Sexiest Women in the World in 2010; her co-star Robert Pattinson (Edward) was named one of the Sexiest Men Alive two years running by *People* magazine (2008 and 2009), and *Vanity Fair* readers voted him the Most Handsome Man in the World in 2009. Both Pattinson and Ian Somerhalder (who plays vampire Damon Salvatore in TV's *The Vampire*

Buffy, Dark Romance and Female Horror Fans
Lorna Jowett

Fig.1: Subverting the male gaze? Buffy *frequently offered male characters as objects of the desiring gaze, as in 'Gone' 6.11*

Diaries [Kevin Williamson, 2009-]) were nominated for the Teen Choice Male Hottie Award in 2012.

Anyone faintly familiar with film theory and gender representation has probably heard of Laura Mulvey's theory about the male gaze of cinema: the male gaze, she argued, renders female characters passive, to be looked at. Mulvey published that theory in the mid-1970s and used Hollywood movies from the 1950s and 1960s as her examples. When *Buffy* first aired, many people dismissed it as a show that displayed pretty teenaged girls for the (implied: male) audience's viewing pleasure in much this fashion. However, *Buffy* had an avowedly feminist creator, women worked on the show as writers, and a few even directed episodes. The show frequently offered a female or queer perspective, visually as well as narratively. *Buffy* certainly presented the bodies of its male characters/actors as objects of desire, showing them in states of undress before the camera equally as much as, if not more than, its female characters. (Naked Spike, anyone?)

Its successors often follow suit. The first *Twilight* (Catherine Hardwicke, 2008) movie had a female director, and it shows. *The Vampire Diaries* airs on the CW, which has a reputation as the pretty boy network. *True Blood* frequently eroticizes and objectifies the bodies of its male characters. Vampire Eric in particular displays his body for the customers of vampire club Fangtasia, and thus for the viewer at home too. A cursory search on the Internet finds masses of publicity images and fan art that repeat this strategy. (This is not to say that the audience for Dark Romance is exclusively female and heterosexual. Rather, as popular culture, it often presents romance, at least superficially, as heterosexual, even while it sets out to interrogate the conventions and ideals of heterosexual romance from a female perspective.)

If the indulgence of a kind of female gaze is one of the female-centred pleasures of Dark Romance, a fantasy of revised masculinity is another. The male characters are often not human, so there is a ready excuse for them to avoid human stereotypes or socially-constructed behaviour. Angel and Spike (*Buffy* and *Angel*), Jean-Claude and Richard (Laurell K. Hamilton's *Anita Blake: Vampire Hunter* novel series, 1993-), Eric, Bill, Sam and Alcide (Charlaine Harris's Sookie Stackhouse novel series [2001-13] and its TV version *True Blood*), Damon and Stefan (L. J. Smith's *The Vampire Diaries* novel series [L. J. Smith, 1991-92: 2009-] and its TV version), and Edward or Jacob (Stephanie Meyer's *Twilight* novel series [2005-08] and the films based on it) all offer a complex mix of traditional masculinity, new man vulnerability and emotional openness and, frequently, metrosexuality. Dark Romance is dark because its male protagonists are powerful and dangerous, often presented as stereotypical bad boys, and the fact that they are vampires or werewolves positions them 'naturally' as predators and their female lovers as prey. But Dark Romance is about subverting 'nature', both monstrosity and masculinity. Otherness in these fictions becomes, over the course of the series, normalized, presenting alternative models of masculinity and femininity, as well as of sexuality.

It is *Dark* Romance also because it shows the flipside of idealized heterosexual romance. One of the most popular, the *Twilight* saga, can easily be read as presenting damaging and/or controlling relationships. Edward's behaviour at times borders on stalking and his watching Bella while she sleeps is either hopelessly romantic or incredibly creepy, depending on your perspective. Vampires Eric and Bill both state that Sookie is 'theirs' in Harris's novels and *True Blood*, and love triangles or rivalries over the female protagonists are a staple of the genre. Such triangles testify to the desirability of the female lead, and allow male characters to flex their literal and metaphorical muscles, but they also present challenges to traditional female passivity. T-shirts with 'Sookie is mine' and 'Sookie is mine now' quotations from Bill and Eric sit alongside 'VILF' and 'Fangbanger' T-shirts in the HBO *True Blood* store. The foregrounding of female agency and of female desire in Dark Romance means that while men, or male vampires and werewolves snarl over who 'gets' the girl, this is not usually how the issue is decided.

Here, when winner takes all, the winner is the 'girl' and she frequently gets all the men. Threesomes feature prominently in adverts for TV shows like *The Vampire Diaries* (usually with Elena looking directly at the camera/viewer, centred in the frame, with Stefan and Damon accessorizing to either side) and Anita Blake acquires a harem of gorgeous male monsters for group sex, a collection of males eventually dubbed 'the Brides of Anita'. While superficially heterosexual (especially on network TV), such triangles and group interactions suggest other possibilities for romance and sexuality.

Moreover, the fact that male protagonists were once traditional horror monsters also indicates a shift away from traditional moral distinctions. Conducting interviews with female horror fans in 2002, Brigid Cherry found that 'Part of the appeal appears to be sympathy or empathy with monstrous creatures' and she argues that many female consumers of horror feel, and enjoy, a 'subversive affinity with the monster'. Repositioning the typical monster as romantic hero changes the game, shifting it closer to the declared interests of these female fans and blurring moral certainty. Milly Williamson points out in her book *The Lure of the Vampire* (2005) that Louis du Pointe du Lac, narrator of Anne Rice's *Interview With the Vampire* (1976), 'like the melodramatic heroine, is virtuous, even as society misrecognises that virtue for guilt or villainy'. Louis, and Barnabas Collins from gothic soap opera *Dark Shadows* (1966–71) before him, is a model for the now hugely popular reluctant vampire figure or VILF. Developing and expanding the trope of the reluctant vampire,

Fig.2: *True Blood* 4.9
'*Let's Get Out of Here*':
*foregrounding female agency
and female desire?*

Buffy, Dark Romance and Female Horror Fans
Lorna Jowett

Buffy featured not only vampire characters like Angel and Spike (both once notorious killers who eventually pursue different paths to redemption), but also werewolves, ex-demons, and witches helping to fight the good fight. Seven seasons of complex morality in *Buffy* seem to have affected subsequent representations to the extent that the reluctant vampire can now be the VILF, the dark hero, the sympathetic villain or a bit of each, as required. Moreover, if contemporary vampire stories and Dark Romance demonstrate that some vampires and werewolves are no longer bad since their 'evil' can be misrecognized goodness, then other things dubbed 'bad' might also become 'good'.

True Blood blatantly flaunts this reversal of received morality with both its tagline, 'Hurts so good,' and its title song, 'Bad things' (Jace Everett, 2005). Anita Blake and Buffy consistently question whether their personal behaviour, especially their enjoyment of violence or sexual activity, is 'bad' and subsequent Dark Romances also follow this lead, interrogating, overtly or implicitly, how women's behaviour is frequently influenced by social norms and outdated assumptions. Even reading or watching explicit sex scenes between female protagonists and their supernatural lovers could be considered naughty – and that's part of the fun. While *Twilight* author Meyer insists that her story is about 'love, not lust' (see Horng 2007), Anita Blake's creator Hamilton emphasizes that her novels are 'sometimes violently sexy' and Carole Veldman-Genz describes the series as 'semi-pornographic'. Cherry's 2002 survey of women horror fans suggests that Hamilton is on the right lines, finding that 'Sexual and erotic themes. […] were important to many' of those she interviewed.

Williamson (2005) argues that vampire fiction is not traditionally considered to be a female form. Yet she also notes how it has merged with 'a range of melodramatic themes and conventions', concluding that these have now become a key part of vampire representation, as seen very clearly in *Buffy*'s soap opera-style narrative arcs and complex character relationships. Some critics, Williamson comments, lament these melodramatic aspects, because they are 'conventionally associated with women's fiction, melodrama and with feminine (and therefore devalued) reading pleasures: the depiction of emotional states and the experience of interior conflicts'. *Buffy*'s focus on its ensemble cast of characters' 'emotional states' and 'interior conflicts' alongside action and horror paved the way for the former elements to take centre stage in subsequent Dark Romances. Though they may still be 'devalued' by critics, they are a hit with audiences, mystifying as this is to some. A *Washington Post* op-ed by Leonard Sax, cited by Catherine Coker (2011), claims that 'the Twilight series' popularity and teen fandom were a revolt against feminism'. Sax is apparently blind to the potential for interrogating traditional models of gender and sexuality through rewriting romance, and fan responses suggest a more complex view of gender representation in Dark Romance. NancyKay Shapiro admits in *Whedonistas!* (2011) that she enjoys writing fanfic about Buffy because she 'could make her play out those romantic fantasies that were maybe all the more alluring to me because they come up to the edge of being "Feministically

Incorrect"'. 'Sexual equality' is picked out by Morehouse (2011) as the elusive 'something that Romance readers and writers were waiting for' and found in *Buffy*, with its strong female characters, sensitive males and continuous, self-conscious blurring of traditional gender divisions.

Whether it's a popular novel series (Sookie Stackhouse, Anita Blake), blockbusting movies (*Twilight*), or in-your-face adult TV drama (*True Blood*) the seriality of these 'sagas' allows for melodramatic elements, unresolved relationship problems, continual deferment of romantic fulfilment and complex character development. The intimate tone promised by the title of *The Vampire Diaries*, while less direct in the TV series than the novels, means revealing characters' personal responses to the action and unfolding plot, as well as the action itself. While Ananya Mukherjea (2011) argues that *Buffy* 'stands apart from' many young adult vampire fictions 'in that the romances in the story are important to the narrative arc but only one piece of it', many Dark Romances follow *Buffy*'s example. Relationships in these series include friendships (Buffy and the Scooby Gang; Elena and her school friends), family ties (Buffy, Joyce and Dawn Summers; Sookie and Jason Stackhouse; Damon and Stefan Salvatore), workmates (Sookie and Sam; Anita and Dolph), and mentors (Buffy and Giles; Bill and Jessica; Alaric and Jeremy) as well as the romantic and sexual ties suggested by the category Dark Romance.

Serial fiction lends itself to an ensemble cast, and these series often feature a group of characters which shifts and changes with the unfolding narrative, and their long-running nature allows for substantial development over time. *Buffy*, for instance, started out like a teen drama, with High School and dating, but it grew up with its characters, becoming darker and more serious over its seven year run. While this may be less obvious in a series that starts out with adult characters it is still evident, and the Anita Blake and Sookie Stackhouse series as well as *True Blood* continually add backstory or extra information about their main characters, as well as introducing new supernatural creatures to keep things fresh.

Mukherjea suggests that

The dominant message in most vampire romances [...] remains a valorization of first loves, an elevation of teenage ardor and teenaged desirability, and of the notion that loving a very good (young) woman can save even an extremely 'bad' man.

This pattern is discernable in the young adult novels she analyses and in some of the teen versions of Dark Romance such as *Twilight* or *The Vampire Diaries*. Yet the long form of serial narrative, the reinventions of gender roles for both male and female characters, the focus on a range of relationships, and, in many cases, the targeting of an older audience, means that much Dark Romance does something slightly different. Dark Romance is not limited to the conventions of romance, nor is it necessarily limited *by* them. When it does deal directly with romance and sexuality, it is able to be self-

Buffy, Dark Romance and Female Horror Fans
Lorna Jowett

conscious about how it uses romantic stereotypes and ideals.

One fan-produced electronic greetings card offered on *BoilsandBlindingTorment. com* presents a soft-focus image of Buffy and Angel from Season 2 of *Buffy* (when they have sex for the first time) with a large title proclaiming: 'Our love is eternal … Just like Buffy and Angel's'. Yet it adds the following qualification as 'punchline':

Well, except that she slept with Parker, what? Four episodes after Angel left? And then there was that whole Riley episode. And I bet she wasn't really thinking about Angel during all that hot sex with Spike, but then again, isn't he all pining for Cordy now anyway when he's not making out with electro-babe?

Sorry, lost my train of thought. What was I saying again?

Since other e-cards in the same section ('cards of love') include messages ranging from 'I hope that I never have to stab you, causing you to be sucked into hell for an eternity of suffering' (another reference to the Buffy/Angel arc of Season 2) to 'Fuck you' (with an image of cave-Buffy from the Season 4 episode 'Beer Bad' [Episode 5]), the notion of romance is not exactly being taken seriously by the site's (apparently female) authors. For those familiar with *Buffy* and *Angel*'s long-term stories, the 'Our love is eternal' e-card serves not so much as it does a criticism of *Buffy*'s plots, as a critique of the entire notion of eternal love. Fans celebrate how the ongoing series played with this sentiment, offering a typical long-form narrative of constantly deferred romantic fulfilment and a series of partners, now seen in the majority of subsequent Dark Romances such as the Sookie Stackhouse novels and its TV adaptation *True Blood*.

In a 2002 interview with Nazzaro, Whedon describes the way denial makes things more interesting: 'No one's going to see the story of Othello going to get a peaceful divorce. People want the tragedy. They need things to go wrong'. The demands of popular serial narrative mean that almost all the Dark Romances follow this pattern, rarely allowing their main characters to be happily partnered for long, or at least deferring the happily-ever-after, and putting numerous obstacles in its way.

Again the Anita Blake series is somewhat unusual in this respect. It provides Anita with 'perfect' partners such as vampire and Master of St Louis, Jean-Claude, and wereleopard Nimir-Raj Micah. Rather than removing one sexual partner and replacing them with another, Hamilton continually adds to the mix of Anita's sexual partners, poking fun at the kind of serial monogamy usually evident in romance. The love-triangles in other Dark Romances fulfil the same function, if in a less provocative manner. In fact, the complicating of romantic fulfilment has reached the stage where *The Vampire Diaries* TV show simply uses the double entendre 'love sucks' as a tag line, invoking in two words Dark Romance's challenge to romantic ideals.

Williamson (2005) reminds us that compulsive (fan) identification has often been identified with the female, and the *Twilight* saga is often mocked or derided precisely because it is aimed at a neglected demographic of girls and young women. Press coverage of the novels and films underscores this negative feminization: an ABC World News story from 2007 describes the author of the *Twilight* novels as '33-year-old Meyer, whose book-signing appearances now draw hundreds of gushing fans' (Horng). In the last few decades, however, TV scholars, commentators and viewers have noted a shift towards complex, character-based drama that encourages, and maybe even requires, long-term viewing by dedicated audiences. Contemporary television drama, as Sergio Angelini and Miles Booy note in 2010's *The Cult TV Book*, is 'marked by the degree to which seriality and other soap opera elements have been embraced as an organizing principle and as a strategy to strengthen viewer loyalty, something once anathema to Network schedulers but now the norm'. In other words, the 'feminized' soap-opera emphasis on relationships and endless continuation noted by Williamson in contemporary vampire fiction has also entered the mainstream of TV. Far from being 'devalued pleasures', melodrama and emotion have become characteristic of quality TV drama. New shows routinely incorporate long-running plot elements, and Dark Romance TV series *True Blood* and *The Vampire Diaries* both have strong season arcs.

When Whedon said in an interview from 2000 that *Buffy* 'was designed to be the kind of show that people would build myths on, read comics about, that would keep growing', he highlights its direct appeal to audiences, to fans, who continue to watch, value and *use* the show. Angelini and Booy describe how a cult text may be consumed by its audience, but it is never entirely consumed, never *used up*, remaining open to new use. Many contributors to the 2011 *Whedonistas!* highlight such use, testifying to *Buffy*'s influence on their own writing of Dark Romance, to how the show helped them tackle personal crises of various types, or to how it changed perceptions of gender, and such stories are replicated across fan sites and discussion boards. That *Buffy*'s influence can be seen across a range of thriving Dark Romances testifies to its success, not just in innovating on well-worn conventions, or providing new ways of representing women, but in packaging 'feminist' ideals in a way that can be popular. Tania Modleski (1996) argued that sales of female gothic mass market novels demonstrated not their female consumers' complicity with traditional notions of gender and romance but rather 'women's extreme discontent with the social and psychological processes which transform them into victims', processes explored in the novels. Likewise, *Buffy* and its legacy of Dark Romance offers serialized stories that, while superficially fantasies of romance, consistently explore its dark side, 'how hard it is to be a woman' for an appreciative female audience. ●

Buffy, **Dark Romance and Female Horror Fans**
Lorna Jowett

~~~~~~~~~~

GO FURTHER

Books

The Lure of the Vampire: Gender, Fiction and Fandom from Bram Stoker to Buffy
Milly Williamson
(London: Wallflower Press, 2005)

Writing Science Fiction and Fantasy Television
Joe Nazzaro
 (London: Titan Books, 2002)

Loving With a Vengeance: Mass Produced Fantasies for Women
Tania Modleski
(New York: Routledge, 1996)

Extracts/Essays/Articles

'How Buffy Changed Television'
Robert Moore
In Popmatters (ed). *Joss Whedon: The Complete Companion* (London: Titan Books,
2012), pp. 140–53.

'Buffy drives home an important issue for women'
Naomi Alderman
In *The Guardian*. 10 February 2012, http://www.guardian.co.uk/books/2012/feb/10/
buffy-issue-women-vampire-slayer.

'Must-See Metaphysics' [*New York Times*, 2002]
Emily Nussbaum
In David Lavery and Cynthia Burkhead (eds). *Joss Whedon: Conversations* (Jackson,
MI: University Press of Mississippi, 2011), pp. 64–70.

'Romancing the Vampire And Other Shiny Bits'
Lyda Morehouse
In Lynne M. Thomas and Deborah Standish (eds). *Whedonsitas! A Celebration of the
Worlds of Joss Whedon by the Women Who Love Them* (Des Moines: Mad Norwegian,
2011), pp. 100–06.

'My Vampire Boyfriend: Postfeminism, "Perfect" Masculinity, and the Contemporary Appeal of Paranormal Romance'
Ananya Mukherjea
In *Studies in Popular Culture*. 33: 2 (2011), pp. 1-20.

'Transgressing With Spike and Buffy'
NancyKay Shapiro
In Lynne M. Thomas and Deborah Standish (eds). *Whedonsitas! A Celebration of the Worlds of Joss Whedon by the Women Who Love Them* (Des Moines: Mad Norwegian, 2011), pp. 69-73.

'Serial Experiments in Popular Culture: The Resignification of Gothic Symbology in *Anita Blake: Vampire Hunter* and the *Twilight* series'
Carole Veldman-Genz
In Giselle Liza Anatol (ed.). *Bringing Light to Twilight* (New York: Palgrave Macmillan, 2011), pp. 43-58.

'Joss Whedon Answers 100 Questions' [*SFX Magazine*, 2002]
Joss Whedon
In David Lavery and Cynthia Burkhead (eds). *Joss Whedon: Conversations* (Jackson, MI: University Press of Mississippi, 2011), pp. 34-41.

'Joss Whedon Gets Big, Bad and Grown Up With *Angel*' [*Science Fiction Weekly*, 2000]
Interview with Patrick Lee
In David Lavery and Cynthia Burkhead (eds). *Joss Whedon: Conversations* (Jackson, MI: University Press of Mississippi, 2011), pp. 14-17.

'That Girl: Bella, Buffy, and the Feminist Ethics of Choice in Twilight and Buffy the Vampire Slayer'
Catherine Coker
In *Slayage: The Journal of the Whedon Studies Association*. 32 (2011), http://slaya-geonline.com/essays/slayage32/Coker.pdf.

'Members Only: Cult TV from Margins to Mainstream'
Sergio Angelini and Miles Booy
In Stacey Abbott (ed.). *The Cult TV Book* (London: I.B. Tauris, 2010), pp. 19-39.

'Will New Bestseller 'Eclipse' Harry Potter?'
Eric Horng
ABC World News. 19 Augsut 2007, http://abcnews.go.com/WN/story?id=3499052#.T2lEKjFOgQA.

Buffy, Dark Romance and Female Horror Fans
Lorna Jowett

'Refusing to refuse to look: Female Viewers of the horror film'
Brigid Cherry
In Mark Jancovich (ed.). *Horror: The Film Reader* (London: Routledge, 2002), pp. 168–78.

Films and Television

The Vampire Diaries WKevin Williamson, CW 2009–)
True Blood (Alan Ball, HBO, 2008–)
Buffy the Vampire Slayer. Seasons 1–7 (Joss Whedon, The WB 1997–2001; UPN 2001-2003)
The Terminator, James Cameron, dir.
(US: Helmdale Film Corporation/Pacific Western Productions, 1984)
Alien, Ridley Scott, dir. (US/UK: Brandywine Productions, 1979)
Dark Shadows ,Dan Curtis, ABC 1966–71)

Websites

Boils and Blinding Torment e-cards, http://www.boilsandblindingtorment.com/card.html

I'VE HAD
MY SHARE OF LOSERS,
BUT YOU...
YOU BOINKED
THE UNDEAD.

FAITH
SEASON THREE

Chapter
7

Seeing Green: Willow and Tara Forever

Kristen Julia Anderson

→ **Their love is everlasting and unstoppable. Willow Rosenberg and Tara Maclay first encounter one another at a UC Sunnydale Wicca club meeting during the episode 'Hush' (Season 4, Episode 10); they soon became one of the most groundbreaking same-sex couples ever featured on broadcast television. Their powerful connection was evident from the start; they were, after all, able to magically move a giant vending machine by just holding hands and making eye contact.**

It was clear there was something between them, something special. Members of the Lesbian, Gay, Bisexual, Transgender and Queer (more commonly known as LGBTQ) community, their supporters, and those who are suckers for any beautiful love story (regardless of what gender the members in the relationship happen to be) couldn't get enough of them. Willow/Tara lasted two and a half seasons; their relationship started tentatively, sweetly and it ended tragically. The two women make mistakes (especially Willow) (see 'All the Way' (Season 6, Episode 6) and 'Tabula Rasa' (Season 6, Episode 8). They fight. They cry. They make their fans cry with them. They separate when Willow, in Tara's opinion, relies too much on 'magicks'. Fans waited for them to get back together when they split up, for love to win. As a couple, Willow and Tara were embraced and often revered by the LGBTQ community; they became more meaningful than even, perhaps, Joss Whedon or *Buffy*'s writers and producers ever anticipated.

In a society where stereotypes run rampant, Willow and Tara served to break down closed-minded misconceptions about LGBTQ individuals and couples. **Their relationship was not sexually exploited or limited to the bedroom – though, ultimately, it wasn't kept out of the bedroom either.** Since the series aired on broadcast television during prime time, limitations existed in regards to how the couple could be portrayed in terms of physical intimacy. In a sense, this worked to the storyline's benefit. As Nicole W. explains in 'Killing Tara: the Demise of an Exceptional Lesbian Relationship on *Buffy*' (2002):

too many television shows have resorted to steamy sex scenes instead of developing the subtle, nuanced verbal foreplay that is such a part of so many relationships because it's just easier to show the characters in bed. Since the *Buffy* writers/producers eliminated this option for so long, Willow and Tara's relationship was allowed to develop at a more leisurely and sensual pace.

Viewers closely experienced both the development of their relationship and Willow's sexuality. In the episode 'New Moon Rising' (Season 4, Episode 19) Willow casually (if a bit nervously) revealed her intimate relationship with Tara to best bud Buffy. The revelation is a bit awkward; with initial, obvious, discomfort on Buffy's part. Buffy soon moves past her shock, reassuring Willow that she is not disturbed by the discovery that her friend is in a lesbian relationship. Tara is also soon fully accepted in the episode 'Family' (Season 5, Episode 6) as part of the Scooby Gang. Episodes such as these convey understanding for LGBTQ individuals who live in a world overrun with sexual discrimination and intolerance. For someone who may be unsure about his or her own sexuality, or wondering if he or she should reveal their own sexuality to a friend or family member, the episodes in which *Buffy* shows Tara and Willow as welcomed by their loved ones are undoubtedly inspirational. When such acceptance is not always guaranteed, seeing a beloved television character receive such desired acceptance is perhaps more meaningful than a non-LGBTQ person can ever understand.

Seeing Green: Willow and Tara Forever
Kristen Julia Anderson

Sexual relationships that fall outside a traditional sphere are often scrutinized. In the late 1990s and 2000s the viewing world was still getting used to seeing same-sex relationships portrayed on network television. In his book *Gay TV and Straight America*

Fig.1: Willow and Tara at the end of 'New Moon Rising' (Writers: Joss Whedon and Marti Noxon, Dir. James A. Contner, Prod. Company Mutant Enemy)

(2006), Ron Becker explains that 'throughout the 1990s, the idea of gay material as somehow inherently controversial remained. No matter how common gay characters became, no matter how successful gay-themed episodes were, the notion that gay material was somehow taboo and risky lingered'. Therefore, this positioning as 'taboo' and 'risky' situated LGBTQ characters as 'unacceptable' to a majority population. LGBTQ characters had little, if any storylines closely based on their lives or relationships. According to 2006's 'Timeline of Lesbian and Bisexual Regular and Recurring Characters on U.S. Television', posted on *After Ellen*, at the time Willow and Tara's relationship was featured on *Buffy* (December 1999–May 2002), they were two parts of the then only thirteen lesbian characters on network television. This lack of central gay and lesbian characters or featured relationships helps to explain why members of the LGBTQ community and their supporters became so attached to this couple.

It also explains the extreme social relevance of the episode 'New Moon Rising', in which Willow's former boyfriend, Oz, returns to Sunnydale in hopes of rekindling their old flame. After Oz left, many *Buffy* fans hoped for his return to the series. And while fans waited for Oz, they met Tara, and like Willow, many fell in love with her. The fledgling relationship between Tara and Willow was cautious, awkward, and also quickly embraced by the LGBTQ community. In response, *The Kitten, the Witches, and the Bad Wardrobe*, an online community dedicated to all things Willow and Tara was formed. It eventually divided into two forums, *Different Colored Pens* (a fanfiction forum) and the *Kitten Board* (a fan forum). The 'Kitten FAQ' explains the origins of the community noting that 'when Tara first showed up on *Buffy* some of us saw the chemistry right away. Shortly a mailing list was created'. The community grew alongside Willow and Tara's relationship. When Oz returned to Sunnydale during 'New Moon Rising', which first aired 2 May 2000, Willow has to choose between him and Tara. The choice, though, wasn't necessarily about her choosing between a man and woman, rather it was about her choosing one person over another person. While she struggled with the decision due to her enduring affection for Oz, she chose Tara because they were falling in love. That's all that mattered; that's all that should have mattered. It wasn't that simple though. The episode aggravated viewers who wanted Willow back with Oz. Many Oz/Willow fans saw Willow as not just choosing Tara over Oz, but saw as Tara converting Willow to lesbianism. Many were seemingly blind to the show's not so subtle previous innuendos which clearly pointed toward a Willow 'coming out' episode. In a post from 'The Bronze' discussion board made on 4 May 2000, Joss Whedon expressed the following:

Okay, let's do this. For real: how @#$%&ing disappointed was I in the American public after Tuesday night? Of course I realize the rabidly homophobic posting contingent represents a smaller percentage of Americans [...] but that's not it. It's the fact that everyone went nuts about it THIS WEEK, when this has clearly been going on for MONTHS? [...] It's the not the bigotry that offends me, it's the lack of filmic insight. Okay, and the bigotry. But of course there were just as many voices raised in support of the arc as against, which was swell. Plus one post from a gay or questioning teen saying the show helped them is worth six hundred hate letters.

Whedon's post speaks to the closed-minded mentality of viewers who were unwilling to acknowledge a relationship which did not conform to traditional male/female pairings. In a television series that frequently challenged definitions of relationships, any instance of discrimination by fans is nothing less than disappointing. As Mary Celeste Kearney notes in her 2007 essay 'The Changing Face of Teen Television, or Why We All Love Buffy', Buffy contrasts 'dramatically with the cheery, wholesome depictions of family life on other early prime-time series, Buffy unabashedly explores identities and lifestyles rarely privileged and often prohibited, by conservative adults'. Therefore the show provided a safe haven for anyone who ever felt like an outsider. 'New Moon Rising' validated the importance of LGBTQ issues by furthering, rather than ending, Willow and Tara's storyline. The episode, though, wasn't about converting anti-gay viewers to a place of understanding (one episode was never going to do that); instead the episode gave a marginalized community with so few televised 'coming out' moments, just one more episode to call their own. In a world of hundreds of 'I choose you' episodes in which a man and woman end up together, 'New Moon Rising' shook the traditional roof off every viewing household and let gay-pride prevail. By doing so, the episode provided much needed inspiration and support for gay teens and young adults. Tara and Willow's relationship was groundbreaking, important, and appreciated by the LGBTQ community of Buffy fans; however, some of the most intimate scenes were left to viewer imagination. At the end of 'New Moon Rising', for example, a moment which begs for a kiss is left to candle flame metaphors.

The show's reliance on symbolism, though, has created a world of opportunity for fanfiction writers. In a 2009 thread titled 'Willow & Tara Firsts' on the website After Ellen, user 'counterpunch' explains that 'while on the one hand I wish they could have shown more firsts on TV [...] it left a nice space for creativity'. Fanfiction writers of Buffy who focus on Tara and Willow's plotline can therefore be seen to further give power and voice to those who may otherwise be ignored within the mainstream. All was not perfect in the world of Buffy and the LGBTQ community though. As Sarah Warn notes in her 2002 article 'Buffy to Introduce a New Girlfriend for Willow?':

Seeing Green: Willow and Tara Forever
Kristen Julia Anderson

Although Willow's two-season relationship with Tara [...], was much-heralded by many in the gay community for its thoughtful and ground-breaking portrayal of a lesbian relationship [...] the series became the subject of severe criticism from many fans [...] when Tara was suddenly killed off.

Yes, other beloved characters were killed off on *Buffy* (see Joyce Summers's storyline); however, characters on *Buffy* returned from death too (see Angel's storyline for example). This was not the case for Tara. In the episode, 'Seeing Red' (Season 6, Episode 19), the couple was romantically rekindling a broken relationship; it was the first episode they were shown bare shouldered and beneath bed covers together. The episode brimmed with happiness and love ... until all was destroyed when Tara was shot and killed by a bullet intended for Buffy. The shocking death scene after such a passionate, loving, sequence devastated Willow and Tara fans, especially those from the LGBTQ community who had found such consolation in the couples' resilience. The decision to kill off Tara, to many, just didn't make sense. However, the 2004 essay 'Girl on Girl Politics: Willow/Tara and New Approaches to Media Fandom' by Judith L. Tabron notes that Whedon claimed Tara's death was a necessary plot device to drive Willow toward her 'dark side'.

In the episodes following 'Seeing Red', Willow Rosenberg indeed travels down a dark path of murderous vengeance and world destruction. Many LGBTQ viewers were outraged at what they considered to be a hurtful and negative message about an intimate lesbian relationship. Specifically, LGBTQ fans were offended that Tara was killed immediately after the show's first non-coded sexual scene between she and Willow and, furthermore, that (the victim's lover) Willow, was portrayed as being driven to blind insanity. Instead of sitting back quietly, fans actively spoke out against the injustice they felt had occurred via online discussion boards and communities. In their introduction to *Undead TV: Essays on Buffy the Vampire Slayer* (2007), Elana Levine and Lisa Parks note that:

The Willow/Tara plot drew broader interest as well, tapping into gay rights discourse and the responsibilities inherent in representing gay characters and themes, particularly when Tara was killed just after having sex with Willow. Fans who had been thrilled to see a sensitive portrayal of a long-term lesbian relationship were angered by the association between lesbian sex and violent death and joined together in a public protest. This story [...] generated grassroots activism to support gay and lesbian youth and question media representation of sexuality.

The Willow/Tara online fan community, *The Kitten, the Witches, and the Bad Wardrobe* is a prime example of the public protest to which Levine and Parks refer. Fans who were outraged over what they considered to be a negative treatment of a lesbian couple took notice and began to actively voice their disapproval. **As noted by several *Buffy***

107

scholars, critics and fans such as Alissa Wilts (2004) and Judith L. Tabron (2004), the violent and senseless death of Tara (and thus the end of the then longest positive lesbian relationship portrayed on television) ignited not only Willow's vengeance, but outrage among fans who considered Tara's death and Willow's lust for blood revenge as perpetuating a negative cliché about lesbians and lesbian relationships. Members of *The Kitten, the Witches and the Bad Wardrobe*, developed a written reaction to the treatment of the couple titled the 'Lesbian Cliché FAQ' (2002). Written by members Kyraroc and Willowlicious as well as other *Kitten Board* members, it presents the negative cliché about lesbians and lesbian relationships as being the 'Dead/Evil Lesbian Cliché'. It is the idea 'that all lesbians and, specifically lesbian couples, can never find happiness and always meet tragic ends. One of the repeated scenarios is that one lesbian dies horribly and her lover goes crazy, killing others or herself'. Therefore, each Willow/Tara story posted at *Different Colored Pens* stands as an active protest against the 'Dead/Evil Lesbian Cliché'; the very existence of the *Kitten Board* and *Different Colored Pens* mark fans' refusal to accept the negative lesbian stereotype they perceive as being presented by *Buffy* writers and producers. The forums are a safe space for LGBTQ individuals who happen to also be *Buffy* fans. In a May 2012 e-mail message, site administrator, xita, explains the social significance of the *Kitten Board* within the LGBTQ community of *Buffy* fans:

The founders [of the *Kitten Board*] are both lesbians who have always had a general interest in [the] gay community [...] The boards were born as a desire to discuss Willow and Tara [W/T] but also because there was, at the time, no real safe space to discuss them. The mainstream *Buffy* places were filled with homophobia, particular desires to get rid of Tara, presumably because she was making Willow gay. The board was a sanctuary where no homophobia could be expressed [...] *Pens* just generally grew, I suppose out of the same desire that has always fueled large fanfic communities, to fill in the (holes). W/T in particular were very coded. For a long time we did not partake in their most important moments as they were coded in subtext and magic. *Pens* brought the text to the subtext. I would say *Pens* was [...] more for W/T fans but that the actual discussion board was more about gay community. A lot of the people who have posted there over the years are people coming to terms with their sexuality through the Willow and Tara experience. My personal commitment is to keep that place open for precisely that reason and keep it free from homophobic remarks.

Discussions about Willow and Tara led LGBTQ fan community members into potentially profound and personally meaningful conversations. When LGBTQ individuals turn to a TV show for support and inspiration, it is no wonder connections are made which others, specifically non-LGBTQ individuals, may never be able to fully understand. To some, the story arc of Willow and Tara was just that – an arc that was necessary for Willow's character – however, non-LGBTQ viewers who have never been persecuted or

Seeing Green: Willow and Tara Forever
Kristen Julia Anderson

marginalized for their sexuality cannot begin to understand the meaning Tara and Willow has had on those who are LGBTQ members themselves. Yes, we all may, at some point, fear we will never find love or emotional connections, but that fear may be intensified for those who find their love discriminated against.

The lack of social acceptance for intimate relationships which fall outside a conventional male/female pairing helps explain why LGBTQ fans of *Buffy* were so outraged by the treatment of Willow and Tara's storyline. Fanfiction provided a means for LGBTQ individuals to tell the stories they want to hear and want to have told. In the '*Pens* FAQ', xita, instructs that

all fics should focus on W/T for a majority of the fic. Angst is very welcome but the end result should be the continuation of the W/T couple, which logically means Willow and Tara are alive and together in the end.

Therefore, by making it mandatory that every fanfiction story posted at *Different Colored Pens* ends with Willow and Tara 'alive and together', all the fanfiction writing posted at *Different Colored Pens* not only serves to rewrite or erase 'Seeing Red' but also presents an active and continual protest against the negative connotations about lesbian relationships fans felt were reflected in the series.

Fans have power, and their power comes through the use of writing as a way to present opposition. Peg Aloi's 2003 essay 'Skin Pale as Apple Blossom' notes the 'level of hurt and indignation among fans [...] who saw Willow and Tara as lesbian role models'. Fanfiction stories then act as wound maintenance and become the voice for positive possibilities denied by the show's writers. Though Willow did ultimately form a new relationship with a potential slayer named Kennedy, after Tara's death, the emotional intimacy she experienced with Tara was not and could never be recreated. Kennedy, was not a replacement for Tara, the two relationships are incomparable, though both have relevance. Willow and Tara presented a romantic, committed same-sex relationship seldom depicted on broadcast television; Kennedy and Willow's relationship was groundbreaking in terms of their physical interactions. Sara Warn explains in her 2003 article '*Buffy* to Show First Lesbian Sex Scene on Network TV' *that*

equal representation of physical affection and sexual interaction between women on television is critical to desensitizing lesbian sex and portraying lesbian relationships as healthy and multi-faceted. The [...] *Buffy* episode does both by treating the Willow-Kennedy sex scene matter-of-factly and including it alongside the scenes of *Buffy's* heterosexual couples having sex.

Despite the strides Willow and Kennedy made toward equal representation of female couples in terms of the physical realm, their pairing was never as deeply embraced by

Fig.2: Willow and Tara
together at the beginning
of 'Seeing Red'
(Writers: Joss Whedon, Steven
S. DeKnight, Dir. Michael
Gershman, Prod. Company
Mutant Enemy)

the LGBTQ community. In fact, mentions of Kennedy are strictly forbidden from stories posted on *Different Colored Pens*.

Willow and Tara struck an emotional and inspirational chord for many LGBTQ fans, which further provides motivation for the stories posted at *Different Colored Pens*. These stories are centered on the positive presentation and preservation of Willow and Tara's relationship. Together, they bring awareness of and attempt to symbolically rewrite the Willow and Tara storyline in a manner that presents it as anti-cliché and as the story LGBTQ *Buffy* fans want to have told and want to hear. Fanfiction stories posted and created at *Different Colored Pens* offer creative active opposition, in the form of alternative narratives thereby giving power to the LGBTQ community of *Buffy* fans.

Fans of Willow and Tara who post on *Different Colored Pens* can be seen as not only extending the couple's relationship, but as also refusing to accept character treatment and portrayals they view as offensive and oppressive. Their relationship may have ended on *Buffy*, but Tara and Willow's relationship lives on in the hundreds of fanfiction stories posted online. Until the time when love is defined not by who is in love, and physical relationships are not scrutinized by the outside observer, online fanfiction communities such as *Different Colored Pens*, at the very least, remain spaces where marginalized character relationships can fully be privileged and embraced. In the realm of *Different Colored Pens*, Tara and Willow will never end, there their relationship is everlasting. ●

GO FURTHER

Books

Gay TV and Straight America
Ron Becker
(New Brunswick, NJ: Rutgers University Press, 2006)

Extracts/Essays/Articles

'Willow & Tara Firsts'
Stephanie B.
AfterEllen.com. March 2009, http://www.afterellen.com/node/46821.

'The Changing Face of Teen Television, or Why We All Love Buffy'
Mary Celeste Kearney

Seeing Green: Willow and Tara Forever
Kristen Julia Anderson

In Elana Levine and Lisa Parks (eds). *Undead TV: Essays on 'Buffy the Vampire Slayer'* (Durham: Duke University Press, 2007), pp. 17–41.

'Timeline of Lesbian and Bisexual Regular and Recurring Characters on U.S. Television'
AfterEllen.com. 2006, http://www.afterellen.com/archive/ellen/TV/Timeline-TV.html.

'Kitten FAQ'
xita
The Kitten Board. October 2005, http://thekittenboard.com/board/viewtopic.php?p=252540#252540.

'*Pens* FAQ'
xita
The Kitten Board. October 2005, http://thekittenboard.com/board/viewtopic.php?p=252541#p252541.

'Girl on Girl Politics: Willow/Tara and New Approaches to Media Fandom'
Judith L. Tabron
In *Slayage: The Journal of the Whedon Studies Association.* 4: 1–2 (2004).
http://slayageonline.com/PDF/tabron.pdf

'Lesbian Type Lovers: Heterosexual Writer Bias and the Dead/Evil Lesbian Cliché in the Portrayal of the Tara/Willow Relationship'
Alissa Wilts
Presented at the *Slayage Conference on Buffy the Vampire Slayer*, Nashville, TN, 2004.

'Skin Pale as Apple Blossom'
Peg Aloi
In Glenn Yeffeth (ed.). *Seven Seasons of 'Buffy': Science Fiction and Fantasy Writers Discuss Their Favorite Television Show* (Dallas: BenBella Books, 2003), pp. 41–47.

'*Buffy* to Show First Lesbian Sex Scene on Network TV'
Sarah Warn
AfterEllen.com. April 2003. http://www.afterellen.com/archive/ellen/TV/buffy-sex.html.

'*Buffy* to Introduce a New Girlfriend for Willow?'
Sarah Warn
AfterEllen.com. December 2002, http://www.afterellen.com/archive/ellen/TV/kennedy.html.

'Lesbian Cliché FAQ'
Kyraroc and Willowlicious, et al.
The Kitten Board. September 2002, http://thekittenboard.com/board/viewtopic.
php?f=7&t=2539.

'Killing Tara: the Demise of an Exceptional Lesbian Relationship on *Buffy*'
Nicole W.
AfterEllen.com. April 2002, http://www.afterellen.com/archive/ellen/TV/killingtara.
html.

Films and Television

'Seeing Red'. Michael Gershman, dir. [2002]. *Buffy the Vampire Slayer: The Complete
Sixth Season.* (US: Twentieth Century Fox Home Entertainment, 2008)

'New Moon Rising'. James A. Contnerm, dir. [2000]. *Buffy the Vampire Slayer: The
Complete Fourth Season* (US: Twentieth Century Fox Home Entertainment, 2006)

Websites

The Bronze Beta, http://www.bronzebeta.com/

The Kitten, The Witches, and The Bad Wardrobe, http://thekittenboard.com/board/

Joss' Comments on Willow/Tara – Bufffyguide.com,
http://www.buffyguide.com/extras/josswt.shtml#ixzz1vjNHkb50

Chapter
8

The Art of *Buffy* Crafts

Nikki Faith Fuller

→ **Anything that inspires people to make their own little version of something be it puppety, be it crafty, be it a high school production of lip syncing, whatever it is, it's the best kind of review you could ever get for any works. It's just cool. I always want things to become plush.**
- Joss Whedon, quoted in 'Joss Whedon on Crafts and Craftiness' (2011)

Joss Whedon's 'peeps' (as he affectionately called his fans in his recent thank you note on *Whedonesque* in light of the success of 2012's *The Avengers*) have been paying tribute to him through gatherings, singalongs, fanfiction, and more since he won our hearts with *Buffy the Vampire Slayer*. The rise of the Internet has provided members of this unique subculture a way to reach out to one another and develop a very special fan base. Starting with message boards and chat rooms, the web presence of Whedon's fans has boomed. Most recently this can be seen in the sales of *Buffy* inspired items such as art, jewellery, clothing and pins on Etsy, the popular website that provides independent artists with an affordable means of selling their imaginative items to niche consumers. Fans have a deeper appreciation for hand-made items than those that are mass produced. The recent rise of handmade items and non-commercial art is evident and has been the focus of works such as Faythe Levine's 2009 documentary *Handmade Nation: The Rise of DIY Art, Craft, and Design*, which emphasizes that these creators have the opportunity to slow down, get hands-on, and move away from big consumerism. As Andrew Wagner of *American Craft Magazine* indicates in the documentary, 'There are so many "things" in the world now that I think people want the things they have in their life to mean something, to have some kind of personal meaning'. And what could mean more to us than items with quotes, images and designs inspired by The Scooby Gang?

It all started with a supernatural Slayer, a gawky teenaged boy and his best friend dressed, as one character callously puts it, by 'the softer side of Sears'. One thing all *Buffy* fans share is love for the characters Whedon and company brought to life on-screen week after week during the series' seven-season run. Many fans like to share how they first met our favourite petite Slayer. In fact, sharing our experiences with each other has become a part of the Whedon experience, and very few of us keep this enthusiasm to ourselves. We urge our friends and family members to watch the show, buy the DVDs, and maybe even join us for a 'Once More With Feeling' (Season 6, Episode 7) singalong. Fourteen Etsy artists were interviewed for this essay, and they all have fond memories of how they met *Buffy*. (Note: all artists will be referred to by their Etsy profile name. Capitalization or lack thereof is true to the spelling on the site. If the artist's Etsy store name is different from their profile name, the store name will be placed in parentheses after the first mention of their name).

Buffy the Vampire Slayer debuted in 1997 when Buffy herself was a young high school student. She captured the attention of many high schoolers at the time and these fans were able to experience all the major teen and early adulthood transitions with the Slayer by their sides. For example, Aleise Lundberg (AMELSEN25) and Jacqueline (weelittlestitches) were in high school when they tuned in for *Buffy*'s debut. Kellie Marion (Krosem Crafts), wookie design and Squeeka have also been devoted fans since the premiere while Karen Hallion (khallion) soon tuned in with the rest of us for Season 2. Megan McFall (Starlight Silver) wasn't far behind; she began watching *Buffy* in 1998 when it debuted in South Africa. Travis Falligant (IBTrav) has a love that stretches back

The Art of *Buffy* Crafts
Nikki Faith Fuller

even further than those of us who were hooked-in when the show debuted – he can claim his fandom all the way back to the 1992 release of the Kristy Swanson film – aka the infamous predecessor to the television series.

Others like WorkingClassVillains and joebot were introduced to *Buffy* the TV series via DVD by the Whedon fans in their lives. Agne Barton-Sabo (BettyTurbo) also discovered the series after it aired. But, as WorkingClassVillains adds, 'it's better late than never'. Lesley (SweetGeek) and lexysaurusrex found *Buffy* on DVD during particularly difficult times in their lives: battling cancer and being hospitalized with appendicitis, respectively. Buffy seems to appear when we need her! Furthermore, even for those of us who were not engaged in a physical or psychological battle when we first met Buffy, we've had her to rely on during hard times over the years, adhering to the popular phrase spawned by Xander's Season 4 speech: 'What would Buffy do?' from the episode, 'The Freshman'. For some of us, it's practically a mantra.

And why do we ask ourselves what Buffy would do? Why did we all keep tuning in, and why do we all keep rewatching it? Because, as Aleise Lundberg mentioned, the series is 'relatable' and deals 'with real issues'. These issues are real to those of us who *weren't* the Cordelia of high school (and let's face it, most of us weren't). The basic situations of each member of the core Scooby gang were not unique: Willow's disconnected mom, Buffy's absentee father, Xander's unhappy parents. Quite simply, they face what we face. For example, Squeeka thought of herself as the 'weird' kid in her seventh grade class when *Buffy* premiered and said at the time, she 'was being bullied pretty badly'. However, she could relate to Xander and Willow, and they became the friends that she 'could always turn to'. As Squeeka has rewatched the series in adulthood, she recognizes 'just how strong those characters are'. The Scoobies also aided Ashley Pitcock in junior high, which she identifies as 'some of the darkest years' of her life. She 'loved how Buffy was a strong, intelligent, and witty woman who faced so many challenges but always overcame them with grace and dignity'. Ashley concludes, 'I feel that watching Buffy helped me get out of those years alive and much stronger than I was before'.

Squeeka addresses the power of the series by identifying, 'Despite all of the vampires and demons and monsters, *Buffy* is about life and death and what it means to be human'. It wasn't the Hellmouth they had to conquer – it was the trials and tribulations and life! Even after graduating high school, the Scoobies face typical struggles: Buffy's out of place at college, Willow loses her first boyfriend, and Xander struggles to find a place in the working class. It was important, of course, as Megan McFall identified, that as Buffy faced difficulties, she 'kicked ass and held her own'! Megan also reminds us that 'there were so few female role models at the time [late 1990s]'. *Buffy* certainly paved the way for strong female characters. The series focused on the empowerment of women – but not just of women, of people. That's the main reason we can all relate to her. In 1997, *Buffy* was necessary, meaningful and timely, and it remains so today. As Travis Fallignant importantly notes, 'Buffy inspires me because I see her as a strong role model. The fact that I am male and she's a female holds no importance. Joss Whedon created a fictional character that one can relate to and care about'.

Agnes Barton-Sabo beautifully sums up a popular response to the series:

There is no guarantee [in Buffy] that all the good guys are going to live happily ever after. It resonates with me because there is no easy answer – no ultimate resolution – things get hard. Then they get harder. There are beautiful moments, but the things Buffy & the gang struggle against are always there. They remind me to keep going. To hold close the friends that make it worthwhile. And the only way to move forward is to be the biggest badass I can be, and just maybe I>ll have time to slay the Big Bad AND make it to prom.

Buffy has inspired us all in surviving our own battles in life. She's connected us in many ways. Most recently, *Buffy* has motivated many fans to create. Most of the artists interviewed for this essay, despite their love and passion for *Buffy*, were not very involved in any *Buffy* communities before they opened their Etsy stores. For some designers like Megan McFall such a community simply wasn't even accessible. In South Africa, she says, 'there is no fan community to speak of'. Etsy finally opened an avenue for her to share her self-claimed obsession. With 368 admirers (Etsy users who have 'favorited' a shop), Megan McFall has finally connected with a community of *Buffy* fans. Though Megan notes that it is of course nice to make money (her art is her living), what she loves the most is 'the fact that there are still so many fans out there'. She continues, 'I smile to think of people wearing my items, and getting to explain what they are to non-watchers of the show!'

All the artists interviewed commented on the importance of community on Etsy. The most common reflection from each artist is that they are happy to find people who love *Buffy* as much as they do. For example, when Lesley discovered that a bracelet she recently sold was being discussed in a fan forum, she reflected, 'Knowing *Buffy* fans like it is really important to me'. These artists are creating something that speaks deeply to them and to their audience; sharing that connection is a prime element in the Etsy world, at least for *Buffy* fans. Wookiedesign even confessed that 'sometimes it's hard to part with something once you've made it just because you're a fan as well. I guess the good thing is I can always make myself something later'. Ultimately, as wookiedesign noted, 'Etsy is great for finding like-minded people'. Agnes Barton-Sabo continues on this idea: 'I think Etsy has established a good reputation of being a go-to place for weird stuff you won't find anywhere else, ESPECIALLY for geeks'. Joebot sums up the general feeling:

Etsy is a great place for fans to come together to celebrate their fandom. I've received so many wonderful e-mails from people who are huge Whedon fans and also happen to really like my work. It's great to see all of the awesome items people create and I love looking through other peoples' shops. Etsy is creativity and commerce at its finest.

The Art of *Buffy* Crafts
Nikki Faith Fuller

This ability for fans to connect with each other by sharing what they love is powerful, and it has even led some artists that started on Etsy to discover other opportunities. For example, by selling her work on Etsy and connecting with fans, Kellie Marion had the opportunity to donate some of her items for a nonprofit event hosted by the *Hellmouth Podcast*.

Joebot has experienced similar opportunities. To begin with, Joebot's love for *Buffy* inspired him to create faux album covers for 'Joss Whedon shows as 1960s kid's albums'. His 'Buffy and the Scoobies: Chosen' has been an Internet hit. Originally designed for his fiancée for Christmas, he later had the idea to sell

Fig.1: 'Buffy and the Scoobies: Chosen' faux album cover © Joebot

it in his Etsy shop as well. In his four years on Etsy, joebot's earned 741 admirers. Success also earned him a spot at Gallery 1988's 'Crazy 4 Cult' art show in Los Angeles in 2010. And in July of 2011 joebot had a design available on TeeFury titled 'Our Lady of Sunnydale'. This image of 'Buffy Summers, the Patron Saint of Vampire Slaying' design is, of course, unavailable on TeeFury now (famous for their motto: 'Tee today, gone tomorrow') but can still be purchased on Joebot's 'redbubble' website (http://www.redbubble.com/people/jo3bot/works/8584576-our-lady-of-sunnydale). Joebot is quite active in the *Buffy* – and extended Whedon fan – communities as well and also donated another piece for auction in the 2011 'Can't Stop the Serenity' charity event.

Working with fans also opens artists to creative collaboration. For example, Megan McFall has received custom requests and recommendations from her customers, including her most recent addition, a necklace featuring a replica of Faith's knife. You can find other great pendants in her Etsy store including 'WWBD?' and Willow's infamous 'Bored Now'.

The culture of Etsy and the art itself on the site are akin to some of the strongest themes emblazoned throughout the Whedonverse: independence, sub-culture and creativity. One great element that stems from this supportive atmosphere is that each artist is unique and has the opportunity to create distinct pieces from whatever materials speak to them.

While most of the artists interviewed were artists first who later incorporated *Buffy* into their work, one exception is lexysaurusrex. She found an Anya quote done in cross-stitching on Craftster a couple years ago (http://www.craftster.org/forum/index.php?topic=299676.0) and was promptly inspired to learn cross-stitching herself. She couldn't imagine a better way to share the wit of Anya. Like the other artists, though, lexysaurusrex does not exclusively sell *Buffy*-themed items. However, many shops do depend on their Whedon pieces for monetary support and popularity. For example, Jac-

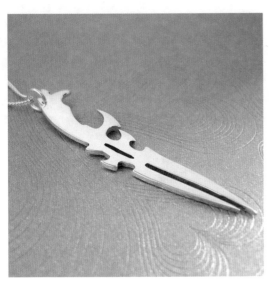

Fig.2: Faith's replica Knife © Megan-Jayne McFall

queline indicates, 'If it weren't for Whedon fans, our shop wouldn't be half as busy'. Likewise, Agnes Barton-Sabo has found that one of her 'insanely' popular items is a birthday card originally commissioned by a customer. It sports Giles saying he'll 'ask the vampires to postpone their prophecy for a few days while you celebrate your birthday'. This guarantees a chuckle from any *Buffy* fan!

As mentioned above, lexysaurusrex learned cross-stitching because she saw a piece she liked. Having a long-tradition in the crafts world, cross-stitching remains a popular choice for artists on Etsy. For example, Jacqueline has been cross-stitching since she was five. She explains:

There's nothing I love more than sitting down with a needle and floss and stitching the day away. There's something so satisfying about making pictures with just a needle and thread. I began designing my own cross-stitch patterns because the choices available for purchase just didn›t suit my own tastes – they were too old-fashioned and too time-consuming. I wanted to stitch something fun and quick which reflected my own geeky interests.

Similarly, Ashley Pitcock prefers to crochet and works in amigurumi, which 'is a knitted or crocheted stuffed toy'. This is something she learned from her best friend and continues to enjoy. After learning to crochet, one of her goals was to learn how to make 'human looking dolls' so that she could 'pay homage to Buffy'. She was happy to take her favourite episodes, 'Graduation Day' Parts 1 and 2 (Season 3, Episodes 21 & 22), and be able to 'memorialize' Buffy with her yarn. Most importantly, she 'love[s] the feeling of producing something that did not exist before'.

Karen Hallion used to paint, but has moved to a method of sketching with a pencil and then editing in Photoshop with a Wacom tablet, a method many modern artists are utilizing. Joebot also prefers to work digitally 'because it's fast and easy to navigate'. Additionally, WorkingClassVillains creates digital art 'inspired by tricks' he's picked up working as a designer for a sign company. Travis Fallignant also works with digital art but has long worked with many other mediums, including watercolour, ceramic, coloured pencil and pen. As a long-time artist and fan of *Buffy*, Travis even won top honours at the 'California State Fair' in the early 1990s for a ceramic figure inspired by the original film featuring Buffy Summers and a staked vamp.

Already a crafter, Kellie Marion made her husband a *Buffy* 'wooden stake' charm for his birthday. After receiving many compliments and requests for more, she began to feature them in her Etsy shop. She shares that in 'two months [they] became the most viewed and best-selling item' in her shop. Sharing a love for *Buffy* and design, her hus-

The Art of *Buffy* Crafts
Nikki Faith Fuller

Fig.3: 'Dammit Joss Whedon'
© Agnes Barton-Sabo

band even started to craft with her.

Megan McFall earned her degree in jewelry design, and an obvious step for her was to bring *Buffy* into her work. She enjoys working with sterling silver, Perspex and resin, and she can also create designs through lasercutting. All of her pieces are handmade. These include, as mentioned above, Faith's knife [IMAGE 2] and 'WWBD?'

Wookiedesign repurposes graphic novels into coasters, frames, clocks, earrings and switch plates. She appreciates the way comics have touched people's lives and designs her pieces to 'give that happy memory back to someone'. To create her work, wookiedesign preserves the original comic print in resin, which lasts a lifetime. Through her, the comic gets to live a second life. She is currently selling switch plates that feature Buffy from the comic books.

Squeeka explains that she 'grew up making things [...]. If I could cut, hammer, bead, glue, paint, or color it, it was fair game'. She enjoys staying in touch with that part of herself. Though she used to be partial to jewellery, she discovered metal stamping several years ago and found her true love. She's 'always been obsessed with putting words on things, and this allows me to do just that'. She loves to tell a story with her pieces, whether it's her own story or someone else's, like our beloved Buffy. Her *Buffy* pieces are stamped with the famous last words spoken after the episode end credits: 'grr argh'.

Aleise Lundberg loves making things that she loves, including magnets, purses, earrings and scarves. If she doesn't sell them, she'll happily use them herself! Similarly, Lesley loves sculpture simply because it's 'fun'. Certainly, all the artists have chosen a medium that they are drawn to and enjoy.

Agnes Barton-Sabo prefers styles of drawing and focuses on portraits. She created an Internet sensation when she designed a print of all the dead Whedonverse characters. She enjoys brilliant colours and quotes and has given us a soulful though humorous look at the loss of Jenny Calendar and Anya, as well as other Whedonverse characters.

A general life philosophy that we can glean from *Buffy* and the art it has inspired has been surmised by Agnes Barton-Sabo: 'Belonging. Inclusiveness. Community, in a very broad and far-reaching sense'. For her, reaching out through crafts says, 'Hey nerds, you're my people!'

Joss Whedon is our people too. He has been successful because he shares his obsessive nerdiness with his obsessively nerdy fans. In his interview with Kim Zerker, quoted at the beginning of this essay, Whedon demonstrates that he is aware of the artistic world *Buffy* has spawned, and he has a deep appreciation for it. On a final note, here are words of wisdom from the man himself from 'Joss Whedon on Crafts and Craftiness':

My advice is what my advice always is: Make stuff. You know. Right now, because of digital technology you can make crafty little movies, you can make crafty little things that go up for millions of people to see [...] [crafts] represent pockets of interaction that an underclass has always used to gather and strengthen each other [to] what's going on in their communities. ●

~~~~~~~~~~~

GO FURTHER

Extracts/Essays/Articles

'The Purple'
Joss Whedon
Whedonesque.com. 9 May 2012 http://whedonesque.com/comments/28797.

'Joss Whedon on Craft and Craftiness'
Kim Zerker
In David Lavery and Cynthia Burkhead (eds). *Joss Whedon Conversations* (Jackson: University Press of Mississippi, 2011), pp. 162–69.

Films and Television

Handmade Nation: The Rise of DIY Art, Craft, & Design. Faythe Levine, dir. (Milwaukee DIY 2009)

Fan Appreciation no.3
Clinton McClung, Founder of the
'Once More With Feeling' touring sing-along

Clinton McClung is a Seattle-based programmer at SIFF Cinema, an organization that screens films year-round as well as produces the annual 'Seattle International Film Festival'. McClung is best known for creating the innovative and engaging interactive event for *Buffy the Vampire Slayer*'s landmark musical episode, 'Once More With Feeling'. The sing-along toured the United States before being unceremoniously shut-down. McClung shares the whole joyous, turned grievous, story here, what *Buffy* means to him, and how a sing-along can be both a connective and liberatory experience for a fan.

Jennifer K. Stuller (JKS): *'Once More With Feeling' is special to me, because after years of ignoring recommendations from friends and family to watch Buffy I finally gave in and it was the first episode I ever saw. As all my loved ones had suspected, I immediately fell in love. How did you come to the series, and what was your experience of viewing 'OMWF'?*

Clinton McClung (CM): I'd actually watched the premiere of *Buffy the Vampire Slayer* – and I didn't like it. I was actually strangely a fan of the movie. Mostly because I was a fan of Paul Reubens. And I went to see that movie in the theatres and it wasn't terrible, it was kinda fluffy, but, I liked it. So I heard they were making it into a TV show and I was like 'WHAT?' and I watched the first episode and I just didn't 'get it'. And then about two years later, I was living in Boston and my roommate and I were flipping through the channels one night and we landed on the finale for season two – and we got sucked into it instantly. And by the end of it, I was balling my eyes out, and was like 'What's happening to me? I don't even know who half these people are! This show is really great!'

That summer they re-ran season two, so I was able to catch up and that's when I got hooked. We would rush home every Tuesday to watch it. Around that same time, I moved in with six girls – in this huge apartment in Boston – and Tuesday night was *Buffy* night. We would just come home and all gather around the TV and I hadn't had an experience like that with a TV show before necessarily, because I'm in movie theatres a lot, so with movies I've always felt that way. And then, to have a show that we all ran home and watched? And then we rewatched it right away? And then talked about it all night? And the next day we watched it again sometimes just to figure out what was going to happen next and how is this character changing? It was one of the first shows I'd seen too, where the characters really evolved. So that's how I got hooked on *Buffy*, and that's how I *stayed* hooked on *Buffy*.

Clinton McClung, Founder of the
'Once More With Feeling' touring sing-along

JKS: *How did you watch 'Once More With Feeling' for the first time? I mean, you must have known there was going to be a musical episode?*

CM: Well, I was a big nerd, so I was the one always reading up on all the fan boards on what's happening next, and I would download the script for every episode and then re-read it ... you know I can't help it.

JKS: *I love it!*

CM: And we saw the ads for the musical episode that was coming up. We heard that he was working on one and we thought, 'Oh my god – this is either going to be *amazing* or *terrible*'. I had no idea, but we were really excited that night. So we all watched it as a group – and *loved* it. We re-watched it three times that night, and that tape did not leave the VCR for like, three weeks. We just watched it all over and over again, and my room-mates and I would catch ourselves singing the soundtrack in the shower, or making dinner or whatever. That's actually how I got the idea to do a sing-along, because me and my roommates would just start bursting into these songs randomly all the time. I'd ran a theatre that had done pro-grams like *The Sound of Music* sing-along and I couldn't help but think, 'Are there more of us, doing this all the time? What if I got them all in a room together? That would be amazing and fun'.

JKS: *Is this the first sing-along that you put together?*

CM: It was the first one I ever pulled together. I'd done other interactive shows, for example, I'm a big fan of mixing variety and cinema. So I would do variety shows, I would have burlesque performers with films. I did a Puppets Night, where I had puppeteers come out and perform between short films. So the idea of not just sitting in a theatre has always been something I've been a fan of.

JKS: *So how did the 'Once More With Feeling' event get started?*

CM: I started programming midnight movies at the theatre I worked at in Boston. If you just program a movie these days, people don't really come. So I was always trying to think of other things to do to attract an audience. So I started hosting as a Mexican wrestler, doing little games before the movies, and I have a lot friends who are artists and performers and we had this theatre so I thought, 'let's do something fun'. And I would collaborate with them on ideas.

In fact, the first Buffy sing-along we did was a collaboration. There was this theatre troupe in Boston that had done a stage play with parody songs called 'Buffy the Vampire Slayer's High School Reunion'. This was while the show was still on the air. It was all the characters coming back together ten years later, and what places they were in – and it was hilarious. I approached them about doing something at my cinema, and the first Buffy sing-along I had, they opened the show by doing a musical number called 'Bite Bite Bite' to the tune of 'Bye Bye Bye' by 'N Sync. It was Spike, Evil Willow and Angel. The sing-along progressed from there.

JKS: *What was the first show like?*

CM: The first time we did the show, I tried to get the rights, clear the rights, to do it in the cinema – nobody would sign off. People at FOX wouldn't return my calls. Nobody knew how to bring a TV show to a theatre – because there are different rights than with a movie. So I just did it as a free show. I didn't charge. I didn't advertise. I just spread the word out amongst the *Buffy* fans. One radio station did a little ad with some giveaways and stuff. And I sold goodie bags, and that helped pay for the use of the theatre that night. Six Hundred people showed up. *Six Hundred people* – out of nowhere.

JKS: *This was at night?*

CM: At midnight.

JKS: *In Boston?*

CM: In Boston. Where there's no public transportation after ten. We were just blown away by the response. It was an amazing screening, everyone was excited. It wasn't right after the musical had aired – that had been around for a year or so. It was around the time the DVD came out for Season 6. So everyone had sort of lived with it and loved it for a little while.

It just blew the doors off the theatre, was fantastic fun, and about once a year or so I pulled it back out and did another screening. And then, I moved to New York City and was working at the IFC Center in the West Village, just doing the boring work, and I was talking to them one night about midnight movies, because they had a midnight movie series and

Clinton McClung, Founder of the
'Once More With Feeling' touring sing-along

it wasn't really drawing people in. So I mentioned the *Buffy* sing-along I used to do, and they thought it was a fantastic idea. I explained the problems I'd had with getting screening rights and they helped me find the people at a company that handles like, not a subsidiary of FOX, but another company that handles rights 'stuff' for FOX. They helped me start to negotiate a deal to actually able to do it in a theatre and advertise it and make it official.

So we booked a screening at the IFC Center. And this was just me this time. I was living in New York by myself. And the show sold out three weeks in advance. They'd never sold out a midnight movie at all before – and to have it sell out three weeks in advance, they were like 'What? What is this?'

JKS: *It's the power of Whedon!*

CM: Totally! The Whedonverse is *huge*! Anyway, it was so popular they started doing it on a regular basis. So once a month we would take over the theatre Friday and Saturday nights, kind of *Rocky Horror* style, and do a *Buffy* sing-along. The first show, I put a sign-up sheet out on the stage and said, 'Hey, I'm doing this by myself. But if there are any other *Buffy* fans in the audience who wanna be a part of this and want to help out sign up!' Something like fifty people volunteered. We had our first meeting that next week and I met all these Buffy fans who wanted to be a part of the show, and we formed a cast out of that. First we had two Buffys, and two Anyas. I had trouble finding a Spike. I always did.

JKS: *Really??*

CM: I think everyone was a little intimated trying to be Spike.

JKS: *And I'm sure you had repeat attendees?*

CM: Yes. Yeah. We had a lot of repeat attendees. We had celebrities come through at one point or another. I never knew they were in the audience and would hear about it afterwards and be like 'What? What do mean Kim Gordon was here with her son? That's amazing!' Because it was in New York, it was just sort of a different game. I did it in Boston for three years before I moved away, and doing the show in New York, and suddenly the *New York Times* called and wanted to do a story on it. *MTV News* sent a crew down and shot a little piece about it, and it just sort of exploded.

I started getting calls from other theatres around the country who were calling asking me how they could book such a thing, and nobody else really knew how to book it or put it together … except for the Alamo Drafthouse.

JKS: *Had you worked with them yet at that point?*

CM: Yes. What's funny is, back when I was working in Boston, Tim League, who is the programmer and the owner of the Alamo Drafthouse, we used to e-mail back and forth a lot just with fun ideas. Because I followed his programming, he followed ours. All the movie theatres, if we're cool, we look at what everybody else is doing. So I'd been communicating with him for a long time, and I'd actually e-mailed him not long after I did the first *Buffy* sing-along and said, 'Hey, I did this thing and it was amazing!' and I sent him all the directions and was like, 'Go with it!' and so they started doing them down in Austin too.
All of this is really sort of fan-oriented. I never really made any money off of doing the *Buffy* sing-along. I made a living doing the tour, but that's because I had to pay for my own flights, and hotels – that was my full-time job for a little while. I also had to pay a lot to the rights owners.

JKS: *Or, who you thought were the rights holders?*

CM: Well, what happened was that the company that had negotiated the rights for me, Criterion, not Criterion the DVD company, a different company that handles FOX's reparatory product, they apparently, thought there was a loophole in their contract that allowed them to do these TV screenings, because it wasn't just *Buffy*, they were licensing other theatres to do *Firefly* marathons, *Simpsons* episodes, *Family Guy*, you know, all this stuff, and they thought there was a loophole in their licence with FOX that allowed them to do stuff on airplanes, that also applied to certain, 'non-theatrical screenings' they called them, which is what they were assuming midnight screenings were. But they're not. We were charging admission and then paying for it. They never told me any of this.

JKS: *Do you think they were just trying to make a buck?*

CM: Yes!

JKS: *And I say that, because in everything that I've read, in prepping to talk with you, you have been so generous in talking about FOX, and it*

Clinton McClung, Founder of the
'Once More With Feeling' touring sing-along

Far Left
Fig.1: Al Lykya and Allexa Lee Laycock reenact Buffy and Spike's kiss at the end of 'Once More With Feeling'. (Photo Credit: Guy Eats Octopus)

Left
Fig.2: Host and Minion agree - it must be bunnies. (photo credit Guy Eats Octopus)

sounded like they really kind of wanted to figure something out, but that Criterion threw you under the bus.

CM: That's what it is, you know, I've never been mad at FOX, because the deal is I think that they didn't know that this was happening.

JKS: *And, well, there are new, weird, legal issues for them to figure out and that takes time.*

CM: And it was so under the radar. I think that Criterion just thought this would be so under the radar they wouldn't even notice. And because I was going through this intermediary I never got an official contract, or anything, all I had was this string of e-mails. I even sent them tour dates with exact days we'd be screening and where and they signed off on them. But it was my own fault that it got shut down.

JKS: *How so?*

CM: It got too popular. You know, doing midnight shows in Kansas City, nobody's gonna care, but going to the 'LA Film Festival', getting a nod in *Entertainment Weekly*, and it wasn't me doing that, it was the fans. Everywhere I played the show, it would sell out. People would go crazy about it, and there would be press about it. And I didn't do anything. I didn't have like a press team, or a PR team.

JKS: *I read in* LA Weekly *that Joss Whedon was at a show.*

CM: That was a total surprise.

JKS: *So tell me about that!*

CM: The LA Film Festival invited me out to do a screening during their festival which I was really excited about. And they said they might try to look into getting some talent or something, but they couldn't get anyone to come out. So I didn't care, I thought it was gonna be fun. I did the whole screening, and right near the end of the show, an usher runs up to me and is like, 'Oh, we have a special guest here'. And I said, 'Oh, really?' 'Yeah, Marti Noxon is in the audience'. So I got up afterwards and said, 'Hey, Everybody! Marti Noxon's here!' She came down and was like, 'Oh, by the way, Joss Whedon is here too!'

Apparently, they'd been sitting in the back row the whole time watching the show, and they wanted to do it kind of incognito so they could see what the reaction was. So, I got to stand onstage with Joss Whedon, and briefly interview him a little bit. You know I'd emailed with his assistant, and tried to connect with him and do something a little more official, but he doesn't have much power over licensing and all that stuff.

He liked the show. He didn't like the 'shut up, Dawn' stuff. (Part of it is, the audience gets way too into that, and I have to rein them in. And that was an audience that was way too into that. The LA crowd was really hating her, and that's why [now] I always try to control it a bit.) The first thing he said actually, was, 'What's wrong with Dawn?'

JKS: *We love Dawn, too ...*

CM: I think part of it, too, is Dawn is his creation. It's hard to hear that people don't like something you created. And it's true – some of the fans just do not like her. I actually kinda, especially in Season 7, I really grew to like Dawn.

JKS: *Yeah, me too. Are you tired of talking about the sing-along after all these years?*

CM: I love talking about it because it was honestly one of the funnest and most rewarding times of my life. Being able to take something that people love so much, and travel around the country with it. Every time I did the show I felt high afterwards, because that audience at every single

Clinton McClung, Founder of the
'Once More With Feeling' touring sing-along

screening I went to – there was so much love in that room. It wasn't for me. It was for what was happening on that screen.

JKS: *But you made that happen.*

CM: No, I *love* being responsible for it. I won't lie about that. But I knew that 90 per cent of the people in my audience didn't know, or give a shit, who I was. That's not why they were there at all. And I always tried to make that a big point of the show too. One of the things I told my Buffy cast, when we first started doing the cast in New York City …

JKS: *And is this 'The Uncool Kids'?*

CM: The Uncool Kids. Yes. They wanted to do it more *Rocky Horror*-style and be on stage the whole time, and I really reined that in, because I didn't feel that that's what *Buffy* needed. *Buffy* needed cheerleaders. We needed to be on that stage to get the people in the audience even *more* excited about what was going on. Not to even be there, or be a presence. So we only came out during the musical numbers, honestly, it was to get people really into the singing. People get into it, and get up and dance!

JKS: *So, kinda building on that, how would you say your fandom in general, or your fandom for Buffy, informs your programming? We've talked about how community screenings and group viewings are really special and enhance the experience. But you also seem, with everything that I've seen you do, to be very generous with it, you want to share it with everybody and not necessarily receive any kind of reward from it – and that's a very fan-thing to do: 'Here. I made this. Enjoy it. Do whatever you want with it'.*

CM: That's always been my goal. Is to not, you know, I'm never the star of the show. The star of the show is the show. And I've never, with a few rare exceptions, presented anything that I didn't have a strong connection to, and I think that's really important. Even if it's something I don't *love*, I *have* to love it for that night. If, I have to, I feed off of the love of the people in the room.

JKS: *That joy is infectious.*

CM: Yes. Exactly. It's the feeling you get from the audience that really informs what you're doing, and not necessarily the show that you're presenting. That said, most of the stuff I do, is stuff that I'm a huge fan of.

JKS: *So there was a petition to save the show – how did that get started? What happened with that? How many signatures were there?*

CM: So, I got the notice that we were shut down, effective immediately. I think this was October of 2009? It seems like yesterday and it seems like forever ago.

JKS: *I remember I'd just heard about them, and then it got shut down.*

CM: Like I was saying, it got too popular.

JKS: *How long did you get to do the tour for?*

CM: Almost a year. I'd actually been travelling a lot. In fact, I'd just finished the first leg of the tour, that I'd printed postcards for, and booked all the rest. And I was planning to go out on the second leg and then also start forming casts in individual cities so people could continue without me. My next goal with the sing-along was not to travel around the country forever. But kind of like *Rocky Horror* was to start little pockets in cities – like Seattle was going to be one of them. Because the shows here were off the hook.

So I was travelling around the country, meeting fans, and working on organizing this. And I'd been building the mailing list over the whole time. And I'd just started booking the second leg of the tour. I was about to go down to Nashville, which we hadn't done before, and I was going to the 'Hawaii Film Festival' in Honolulu. Then I got the call that it was cancelled. Effective immediately I had to cancel all the future bookings. I'd already spent a bunch of money on airplane tickets and stuff. It *sucked*.

JKS: *So Criterion called you?*

CM: Yeah. And what happened is they had gotten a call from FOX who were wondering what this was about and why they'd authorized it, because FOX hadn't. They had to pull the plug right away, and blamed me for everything. Publicly. Even though it was nothing I did. I'd gone through them, like I was supposed to. So in New York we decided to start a petition. Because people were emailing me right away. So we started an on-

Clinton McClung, Founder of the
'Once More With Feeling' touring sing-along

line petition for people to sign and say, 'We really want the sing-along to continue'. I hired an entertainment lawyer to look into working with FOX to get the rights cleared and make it happen. Ultimately, what it all came down to was somebody complained to FOX. I think somebody from SAG, the Screen Actor's Guild, or somebody who was supposed to be getting residuals for the show, that this wasn't in their contract that they could do theatrical screenings and where was their share of this? I never really found out what happened. But because we started getting some national attention, FOX got a call about it.

JKS: *Did you get hit with having to pay those residuals?*

CM: No. I had been paying Criterion for these screenings. So my lawyer told me not to pay them anymore and just stop. But I was out airfare, and I had just bought a bunch of props for the second leg of the tour, so I had a bunch of *Buffy* stuff in a closet that I didn't know what to do with.

JKS: *Ebay?*

CM: Well, I started to put together little home party kits – which were all of the props you would need for you and fifteen friends, and some trivia. Everything but a copy of the show.

JKS: *Okay – Etsy.*

CM: I used to sell them on Ebay.

JKS: *You should sell them on Etsy. I'd totally buy one.*

CM: I did that because it wasn't just the show that was shut down. It was like, 'Boom. You're unemployed'. That had been my whole life for nine months.
   Anyway, so we started the online petition and I think ultimately it was 68,000 signatures. I gave that to my lawyer to give to FOX, and we just never got them to do anything with it. I think part of it is, and I don't blame them for this, but in order to make the show happen theatrically, like, in a movie theatre, they would need to redo *every* contract. And not just that episode, but the whole show. And I think that ultimately would have cost them millions of dollars. And you know, the *Buffy* sing-along was hugely popular, but it made them thousands of dollars. It was nothing they ever thought of as something to really release out there and make a lot of

money off of, but I'm sure if that were the case, they would have gone for it. Or, would have taken the idea, you know, taken what I created and just done it – which was always a possibility too.

JKS: *Well, but it wouldn't have been as charming.*

CM: Well, and as I told my collaborators when other Buffy sing-alongs started popping up – 'Whatever! We don't own this. It's fan based'. The only reason I was doing the Buffy sing-along tour was because people in other cities weren't organizing them. If other people were organizing and made it happen – I was fine. (But, then I did get a little anal, because I thought mine was perfect.)

JKS: *Naturally.*

CM: I changed it every time I did the show. Like, I was always adding a little element, or responding to what I thought the audience really liked. That's where *Buffy*oke came from.

The episode is only an hour. When we originally started doing it, we'd show the episode and then show another episode after. But I always felt that, even though it's fun to watch Buffy with a crowd, it was always a little bit of a letdown after doing the musical. Everyone's pumped up, and then you show 'Pangs' and everyone cries. Or, you'd show 'Smile Time' from *Angel*, which was fun.

Showing two episodes wasn't really working for me, plus, since it was a midnight show, it wouldn't be over until like 2.15 in the morning. So, Henry, down at the Alamo, was doing a thing he called Cine-Oke, which is also done at other places in the country. It wasn't karaoke – it was people reacting to movie scenes in front of the screen. So he started doing that with Buffy – and I thought that was a great pre-show activity. So I picked three or four scenes from the show. We always did the scene – it was either from 'Surprise' or 'Innocence' where Buffy returns to Angel's lair and finds that he's evil now, and he's totally mocking her for sleeping with him the night before. We always did that, because there's so much drama in a one-and-a-half minute scene. It's amazing. But we always flipped genders. I'd call up two people to be on stage, and then say, 'You're Angel – and you get this blonde wig to be Buffy'. And it was so fun. The guys loved being Buffy in that scene. And the girls loved being Angel.

So what we would do is we would play the scene through once, watch it with the captions on. And then we'd play it with no sound, and then they

Clinton McClung, Founder of the
'Once More With Feeling' touring sing-along

had to act out what was on the screen. And people loved it. It was so fun to do. I had one with Giles singing …

JKS: *Oh – 'Behind Blue Eyes'?*

CM: No. I had him signing the exposition song from the dream episode.

JKS: *'Restless'.*

CM: Yes. That one would get the whole audience into the singing. I had one for 'Doppelgangland' with Evil Willow meeting Sweet Willow and seducing her. The girls liked to do that one!

I put together some trivia video montages – so instead of reading trivia, I'd show a clip – those were really fun. I'd go on YouTube and find fan videos that were just awesome. I mean, some of them were terrible, and some of them were awesome. So we would have a half-hour of stuff beforehand to lead into it. I always did *Buffy*oke last because it got the audience excited.

JKS: *Tell me how you filtered back into being able to do these.*

CM: Well, doing it at conventions is different than doing it theatrically. You're not charging anybody just for the screening. You're not making any money off of it really. Fan screenings or TV shows, even the huge Comic-Con [International] – they're doing stuff like that. Because that's not a huge licensing issue. It's different to have a show in a movie theatre and advertise it.

And I did think briefly after everything was shut down of trying to do it at conventions and, I'm not the first person to ever think about doing a sing-along to *Buffy the Vampire Slayer*. And it had been done at some fan conventions before – I'd never been to one, but I'd read about them. I used to be more blunt about this, but I changed my tune a little bit. I just don't like the vibe at those Cons. One of the things I really loved about doing the sing-along and doing it in the theatres, was that there would be so many people there, and this is their only chance to really celebrate *Buffy* in the public sphere. They're not as huge nerds, as wanna go to a convention, they're a little more casual lovers of it. But that experience, in the theatre, that one night, is almost transformative.

I've met so many people at sing-alongs, ages 8–80 – seriously – sometimes in the same crowd. But I had so many people who walked up to me after and said, 'I never watched this show before. My friend dragged me to this screening and it's *amazing*'.

And that's one thing that Whedon actually said in an interview one time was that he didn't see how people could watch this out of the context of the show, and I totally disagree. You can watch 'Once More With Feeling', not understand what the characters' motivations are, or know about the mythology or anything, the songs are so good, the vibe is so awesome; it really has an emotional arc that pays off at the end.

JKS: *As my first episode, I fell in love with it, and then going back after watching the whole series and rewatching it, you have a deeper experience. Like when Xander's singing about marrying a 'demon' – that works on many levels.*

CM: I think the reason it works so well, is because Whedon had been wanting to do a musical episode since Season 1. He'd been storing up all these ideas and themes and stuff, to really bust them out at the right moment. And it works so much – it's almost a stand alone episode.

And I like to say whenever I host a show, that tonight is the night you let your freak flag fly. There is nobody in this room that is going to judge anything you do because we're all gonna do it too.

~~~~~~~~~~

GO FURTHER

Websites

Once More With Feeling: The Buffy Musical, http://uncoolkids.com/buffy/

Chapter
9

*Buffy*verse Fandom as Religion

Anthony R. Mills

→ **But I guess the thing that I want to say about fandom is that it's the closest thing to religion there is that isn't actually religion.**
- Joss Whedon, *Wired*

Fig.1: The season four episode 'Superstar' is a reference to every Buffy fan's fantasy of being part of the Scooby Gang. Credit: Superstar, written by Jane Espenson, directed by David Grossman, 2000, © Twentieth Century Fox

Arguably more than any other television creator, Joss Whedon is aware of the intense devotion of his fans. Even as an avowed atheist, he recognizes the similarities between fandom and religion; likenesses which no doubt have contributed to his success, for only the truest believers have followed him from hits like *Buffy* to failures like *Dollhouse* (2009-2010), from obscurity to what will surely be household popularity after *The Avengers* (Joss Whedon, 2012). Yet what if we remove any notion of the supernatural from our idea of what religion is? Could we then talk about how fandom is not only *like* religion, but that it actually functions *as* religion?

One would think that the first hurdle, of course, is to define what we mean by 'religion'. This daunting task is akin to that of St Augustine when he acknowledges the difficulty in discussing the concept of time in his spiritual autobiography, *Confessions* (AD 397 and AD 398): we all know what it is until we actually have to talk about it, at which point we are at a loss. Following his lead, we will proceed not so much by saying what religion *is*, but rather, more fluidly, what it is *about*. It is, after all, the sheer pervasiveness of religion which makes any definition immediately problematic. One can see this in the works of Whedon, who, although an atheist, consistently promotes ethical and philosophical positions which have their origins in specific religious traditions and beliefs in the supernatural. That old-time religion does not go away easily.

Over the last two decades, a new approach to religious studies has emerged which can help us shed light on this tenacity of religiosity. Using the tools of both the natural and social sciences, the cognitive science of religion, also called the biocultural science of religion, has discovered the deep biological structures and impulses which have contributed to the formation of both traditional religion (for example, Islam, Christianity, Greek mythology) and contemporary religion, such as pop culture fandom.

While most researchers in this field argue, against our thesis, that some belief in the supernatural is essential to what we call 'religion', all of them posit that religious phenomena have their basis in fundamental biological and psychological processes. It is primarily for this reason that Loyal Rue named his helpful book on the topic *Religion is Not about God* (2005). Aside from the problematic dichotomy of natural/supernatural, which is a western construct not found in all world religions, Rue argues that religion is ultimately about human beings anyway. Specifically, religion has to do with manipulating our brains for the sake of both personal wholeness and social coherence. Or, to put it more colloquially, religion is about being a part of something bigger than oneself in a way that is also personally fulfilling.

*Buffy*verse Fandom as Religion
Anthony R. Mills

In the remainder of this chapter, we will explore this general human life strategy in several specific ways it comes to expression in *Buffy*verse fandom. In so doing, we will flesh out in more detail how the cognitive science of religion acts as a helpful dialogue partner for understanding what it is about Buffy's world which makes it so damn appealing.

The first and most overarching observation is that *Buffy*verse fans are *emotionally* committed to the show (*Buffy the Vampire Slayer* and, often, to its spin-off series *Angel* [Joss Whedon and David Greenwalt, 1999-2004]) and to the fan community itself to a degree rarely found with other media texts. The power and importance of emotions are not lost on Rue and others working in the cognitive science of religion, despite the common association of 'cognitive' with 'rational' and thus opposed to 'emotional'. Although the cognitive/emotional opposition is another problematic dichotomy, some prefer the term 'biocultural science of religion' to avoid any confusion. What is meant by 'cognitive' here is actually that which has to do with the brain and its functions, which includes emotionality. It is primarily by manipulating the emotions that religions of all kinds hold sway over their adherents. Even the very word 'fanatic', of which 'fan' is a shortened form, implies intense emotionality, even religious fervour, which is precisely how it came to be understood in very early Latin ('fanaticus') and eventually in English also. Some even suggest that emotional commitment is precisely what differentiates fans from non-fans or casual viewers.

Indeed, Michael P. Levin and Steven Jay Schneider assert in their 2003 essay on *Buffy* that the show's success depended on its 'ability to entertain and engage viewers *psychologically*'; that is, through the emotions (original emphasis). It is largely for this reason that, when asked, *Buffy*verse fans often have difficulty articulating why it is that they love the shows. There is an emotional dynamic which precedes one's ability to coherently formulate their appeal in terms of rational discourse. This is in no way to suggest that fans' feelings of attachment are then *irrational*, merely that fandom, like traditional religions and many other human phenomena, elicit emotional responses which come before and in fact beg reasons for them.

One of the chief reasons for the intense devotion of *Buffy*verse fans is the importance of community for both the characters in the shows and among fans themselves. As we mentioned above, the pursuit of social coherence is one of the main goals of human behaviour, for which religion in its various forms acts as a mediator toward that end. Some have gone so far as to argue that religion is in fact the strongest social bond of all and that among very early human communities, those with a shared religion (including a shared belief in the supernatural) would have cohered better than those without. This is certainly true within the narratives of both *Buffy* and *Angel*. What brings the 'Scooby Gang' together most forcefully in the very first episode is the shared belief in vampires, demons and monsters, which is mostly why those who are not willing to believe in these creatures remain very much on the periphery of both the show and the principal characters' lives. In *Angel*, similarly, it is the belief in the supernatural powers of darkness which set the core group off from others.

Yet what keeps these communities together is not the shared belief as such, but how they respond to it. The awareness of demons and vampires provides the catalyst and limits their field of intimate friends, but it does not demand that they care about each other. Rather, it is when this awareness is accompanied by a recognition of powerlessness in the face of it that true community happens. In other words, only when each member of the gang realizes that they cannot handle life alone, especially life in a world infested with demons, do they really come together. In every instance where internal suffering is kept from the group, community breaks down despite the shared belief system. This is precisely why Jonathan, for instance, never becomes part of Buffy's group, in spite of his seeming awareness of the vampires; he never lets himself be really vulnerable.

In a great irony, it is this aspect of the *Buffy*verse which makes it more religious than religion, as it were, at least in contemporary western culture. According to most biocultural science of religion scholars, the reason that religion bound early communities together was chiefly because belief in supernatural moral agents put limits on unwanted behaviour. For instance, studies show that people are much less likely to cheat and steal, even when no other people are around, if they think that an invisible force is watching them, such as a god or spirit. Some even see this as the very reason that deities were invented in the first place; as a psychological restriction on criminal and taboo behaviour. Even today, many religious people manipulate others, especially children, by telling them or suggesting that God will punish them or is punishing them for some kind of moral transgression, whether it be lying, having sex outside of wedlock, being gay or even not attending worship anymore.

In the contemporary West, however, such threats carry consistently less weight because people have the option to pursue social relations which are not so psychologically abusive. To the extent that Rue is right that people want social cohesion as well as personal fulfillment, this is coming to expression in a yearning for genuine intimacy and vulnerability, such as seen between the characters in the *Buffy*verse. In this sense the *Buffy*verse is more religious than traditional religion because it is more genuine and respectful of others' uniquenesses and flaws.

At the same time, it is widely acknowledged that real intimacy and hence fulfillment are wildly allusive in western culture. Freedom from our ancestors' religious restrictions has brought with it freedom from anything of real commitment and depth. As Henry Jenkins insightfully observes regarding cult shows in his 1992 book *Textual Poachers*:

The fans are drawn to these shows precisely because of the vividness and intensity of those relationships; those characters remain the central focus of their critical interpretations and artworks. Life, all too often, falls far short of those ideals. Fans, like all of us, inhabit a world where traditional forms of community life are disintegrating, the majority of marriages end in divorce, most social relations are temporary and superficial, and

*Buffy*verse Fandom as Religion
Anthony R. Mills

Fig.2: 'Family', from season five, challenges the normativity of the nuclear household as Tara is taken in by Buffy and hew crew. Similarly, religion and fandom both are attractive because of the sense of belonging offered to the outsider. Credit: Family, written by Joss Whedon, directed by Joss Whedon, 2000, Twentieth Century Fox

material values often dominate over emotional and social needs.

It is not only traditional religious institutions which fail at genuine community, but the family as well. Aside from Buffy's relationship with her mother Joyce, which ends with Joyce's death in Season 5, there is no other significant biological bond which ties the characters together. Dawn, of course, is eventually found to not be Buffy's sister. Over on *Angel*, the only close family connection is that between Angel and his son Connor, which lasts for just over a season until Connor is essentially sent away to live with an adoptive family. Yet both the Scooby Gang and the group at Angel Investigations are consistently presented as families; with all the bickering and misunderstanding come genuine care, grace and self-sacrifice.

When we consider the importance of the nuclear family in television shows of previous generations, the shift away from it is significant, marking the perennial turn toward isolation and abandonment which characterize western life. Much of Whedon's success in fact exploits such feelings because people still want to be part of something larger which contributes to personal happiness. We should bear in mind as well that traditional religions have offered themselves as alternative forms of family just as much as they have as institutions which come alongside and strengthen the family. In an era where both consistently fail to assist in the twin goals of social cohesion and personal wholeness which Rue mentions, something else arises to take their place. For many, that something consists of various cult media and their fans.

In a world where traditional religion and family are still considered mainstream and thus normative, pop culture media and fandom take on something of a minority or ostracized status. In the *Buffy*verse narrative itself, characters experience this in two major ways. The first is the rather mundane fact, shared by many viewers no doubt, that the authorities and institutions which they are supposed to trust turn out to be irrelevant, disinterested or corrupt. Consistently over both series, most parents, teachers, school officials, bosses, political and religious leaders, and police and military authorities are clueless, helpless or outright villainous and antagonistic to Buffy and Angel and their crews. This trope of the adolescent power fantasy is common in films and series aimed at teens, who are in the precarious position of possessing physical and intellectual ability but are limited by legal restrictions. In Whedon's works, however, the use of this formula seems more self-consciously aimed at the fans who find themselves in the same position of cultural obscurity.

The second way is through their very knowledge of the demons, vampires and monsters which plague Southern California and threaten the world. Such secret or esoteric knowledge contributes greatly to group commitment, according to cognitive science of religion, especially when this insight is of a dangerous or apocalyptic nature. It is precisely because of its power to cohere groups together that most religions tend to be exclusivist and claim a special knowledge of the divine. This power is intensified whenever religious groups feel oppressed by the larger culture, which is a major reason that dangerous cults like the Branch Davidians and Heaven's Gate continue to exist. This is not to say that Buffy's Scooby Gang (or fans for that matter) qualifies as a cult, but shared exclusion does help to make sense of why the group stays together in spite of a few fairly drastic personality differences. It is not merely a narrative contrivance, but also an anthropological tendency.

Strangely, it is partially the same horror elements of the shows which give *Buffy*verse fans something of an outsider status as well. Vampires, monsters and demons are not mainstream fiction elements, so their fans tend to be part of a niche group (or, one could argue, their prior shunning by more socially acceptable people influenced their interest in the horror genre). In any case, it seems that for *Buffy*verse fans, the hook is the feeling of being a part of a misunderstood group and the concomitant excitement of sharing that with the select few who also 'get it'. Just as having an inside secret or marginalized standing strengthens religious groups, for many fans it is the experience of being different from the majority which facilitates genuine community.

Three phenomena in particular undergird the parallels between traditional religion and *Buffy*verse fandom and highlight the outsider status of each. The first is the unique use of language in both. Anyone who is part of a traditional religious community recognizes that there are terms used in and about worship which are either never said or mean something quite different in a mundane context (e.g. 'glory', 'praise', 'Hallelujah', 'testimony'). There are also obscure theological terms which mean nothing except to those who study such things by profession or for leisure, even transcending the knowledge or interest of the average worshiper (e.g. 'atonement', 'transubstantiation', 'perichoresis'). In terms of biocultural science of religion, proficiency in such terms acts as a cost-signalling mechanic whereby devotees communicate to others that they belong solidly to a particular religion and perhaps even to a particular sect or denomination therein.

Because of Whedon's unique use of language in several of his shows, *Buffy*verse fans also demarcate themselves by the use of slang, and for the same purposes. In his 2009 study of online *Buffy*verse fans, Asim Ali found that the use of special lingo was so pervasive that deciphering what was actually being said was difficult for the novice. Moreover, lingo was so important for these fans that conventional use of language was often the exception rather than the rule. We can understand slang among fans in the same way that religious language works for worshipers; the more it is used, the more it signals group commitment to others and also serves to distinguish non-fans and casual viewers from devout fans.

The second parallel has to do with ritual. According to Nicholas Wade, religions strengthen moral and emotional attachments through ritual, a feature which less cohesive groups lack. As creatures of habit, human beings are naturally inclined to repetitive behaviour, which in a religious setting helps to solidify beliefs, behaviours and thus

*Buffy*verse Fandom as Religion
Anthony R. Mills

commitment. *Buffy*verse fandom also includes rituals, such as repeat and communal viewings, attendance at conventions, intentional use of slang, and regular times of on-line discussion. In both cases, rituals serve to propagate the original myth, often far beyond its end. Just as Christianity would have most likely died out without the systematic remembrance of Jesus through the rituals of baptism and Eucharist, so too would *Buffy* and *Angel* be little more than old television series were it not for the fan community which still brings vitality to the *Buffy*verse through various practices.

One of the major ways this happens, thirdly, is through fan-made art, fiction, videos and comics; *Buffy*verse fandom, like other cult media fandoms, is thoroughly participatory. In this regard the connection between fandom and traditional religion is a bit more tenuous. Religious establishments secure themselves against heretical beliefs and practices (i.e. against outsiders) precisely by defining what counts as right doctrine, rituals and emotions and by controlling how these are expressed in worship. In other words, religious leaders define the canon or 'official' religion. In media culture, the closest analogue we have to the religious authorities consists of the creators, producers and studio executives who define the canon of any given media text.

*Buffy*verse fans, however, like the *Star Trek* (Gene Roddenberry, 1966-69) and *Star Wars* (George Lucas, 1977) fans before them, rebel against the official canon and thus the creators by writing stories differently or by creating new stories with their beloved characters. This is not merely done in private, but within the fan communities, where members share art, literature and videos with each other, more and more in plain sight of the official creators who control the legal and thus financial rights to the mythoi and characters.

This subversion is much more difficult to accomplish in a traditional religious context because the authorities' need to control matters of dogma and ritual concern more than just money; emotional attachments and social cohesion are also at stake. This is not to say that religious people do not deviate from institutional norms and expectations, but they tend to do so privately. Nevertheless, in our current cultural context where religious adherence is not restricted by law, the similarities between religious and cult media rebels may be greater than we first saw. If we consider the multitude of schisms and offshoots which characterizes the western religious landscape, the subversion of official authority by religious people is much closer to that of *Buffy*verse fans; a canon is recognized, but it is not the exclusively binding authority for the propagation of the myth. In some cases, a new canon or even the refusal of a canon is required.

The notion of *Buffy*verse fandom as religion which has been sketched out has its limitations and will certainly have its detractors. Certainly more needs to be said about the differences, especially those concerning belief in supernatural forces. Nevertheless, if we are open to a broader understanding of religion, particularly one which is informed by cognitive or biocultural science, its similarities to pop culture fandom merit further consideration and investigation. ●

GO FURTHER

Books

The Faith Instinct: How Religion Evolved & Why It Endures
Nicholas Wade
(New York: Penguin, 2009)

Evolving God: A Provocative View of the Origins of Religion
Barbara J. King
(New York: Doubleday, 2007)

Religion is Not about God: How Spiritual Traditions Nurture our Biological Nature
Loyal Rue
(New Brunswick: Rutgers University Press, 2005)

Fan Cultures
Matt Hills
(London and New York: Routledge, 2002)

Textual Poachers: Television Fans & Participatory Culture
Henry Jenkins
(New York and London: Routledge, 1992)

Extracts/Essays/Articles

'Joss Whedon on Comic Books, Abusing Language and the Joys of Genre'
Adam Rogers
Wired. 3 May 2012, http://www.wired.com/underwire/2012/05/joss-whedon/all/1.

'Introduction'
Mary Kirby-Diaz
In Mary Kirby-Diaz (ed.). *Buffy and Angel Conquer the Internet: Essays on Online Fandom* (Jefferson, NC and London: McFarland, 2009), pp. 1–6.

'Buffy, Angel, and the Creation of Virtual Communities'
Mary Kirby-Diaz
In Mary Kirby-Diaz (ed.). *Buffy and Angel Conquer the Internet: Essays on Online Fandom* (Jefferson, NC and London: McFarland, 2009), pp. 18–41.

*Buffy*verse Fandom as Religion
Anthony R. Mills

'"In the World, But Not of It": An Ethnographic Analysis of an Online *Buffy the Vampire Slayer* Fan Community'
Asim Ali
In Mary Kirby-Diaz (ed.). *Buffy and Angel Conquer the Internet: Essays on Online Fandom* (Jefferson, NC and London: McFarland, 2009), pp. 87–106.

'Community, Language, and Postmodernism at the Mouth of Hell'
Asim Ali
In Mary Kirby-Diaz (ed.). *Buffy and Angel Conquer the Internet: Essays on Online Fandom* (Jefferson, NC and London: McFarland, 2009), pp. 107–25

'"Easy to Associate Angsty Lyrics with Buffy": An Introduction to a Participatory Fan Culture: *Buffy the Vampire Slayer* Vidders, Popular Music and the Internet'
Kathryn Hill
In Mary Kirby-Diaz (ed.). *Buffy and Angel Conquer the Internet: Essays on Online Fandom* (Jefferson, NC and London: McFarland, 2009), pp. 172–96.

'The Cognitive and Evolutionary Roots of Religion'
Scott Atran
In Patrick McNamara (ed.). *Where God and Science Meet: How Brain and Evolutionary Studies Alter Our Understanding of Religion.* Vol. 1. *Evolution, Genes, and the Religious Brain* (Westport: Praeger, 2006), pp. 181–207.

'Amazing Grace: Religion and the Evolution of the Human Mind'
Ilkka Pyysiäinen
In Patrick McNamara (ed.). *Where God and Science Meet: How Brain and Evolutionary Studies Alter Our Understanding of Religion.* Vol. 1. *Evolution, Genes, and the Religious Brain* (Westport: Praeger, 2006), pp. 209–25.

'Feeling for Buffy: The Girl Next Door'
Michael P. Levin and Steven Jay Schneider
In James B. South (ed.). *'Buffy the Vampire Slayer' and Philosophy: Fear and Trembling in Sunnydale* (Chicago and LaSalle: Open Court, 2003), pp. 294–308.

'www.buffy.com: Cliques, Boundaries, and Hierarchies in an Internet Community'
Amanda Zweerink and Sarah N. Gatson
In Rhonda V. Wilcox and David Lavery (eds). *Fighting the Forces: What's at Stake in 'Buffy the Vampire Slayer'* (Lanham: Rowman & Littlefield, 2002), pp. 239–49.

'Buffy, the Scooby Gang, and Monstrous Authority: *BtVS* and the Subversion of Authority'
Daniel A. Clark and P. Andrew Miller
In *Slayage: The Journal of the Whedon Studies Association*. 1: 3 (2001), http://slayageonline.com/PDF/clark%20_miller.pdf.

Fan Appreciation no.4
Scott Allie, Dark Horse Comics

Photo by Jessie Christiansen

Scott Allie is an editor and writer, and currently Senior Managing Editor at Dark Horse Comics. Allie is intimately involved in the production of *Buffy the Vampire Slayer Season 8* and *Season 9* comics – a groundbreaking project that has changed the game for transmedia storytelling. He shares how *Season 8* got started, reactions from fans, and what's gratifying about the *Buffy*verse.

Jennifer K. Stuller (JKS): *How did you first come to be involved in the Buffyverse, and in particular, the production of* Buffy *comics? Were you a fan of the show?*

Scott Allie (SA): I was not. I hadn't seen the show. We'd acquired the licence, near the end of Season 2, if I recall, and I heard the word 'Vampire' in the title, and, being a fan of the horror genre, jumped at it. I didn't watch much TV at the time, or I probably would have already checked the show out for the same reason.

JKS: *How did Dark Horse come to take on the* Buffy *comics, and what was the process that led to the groundbreaking, and trendsetting,* Buffy the Vampire Slayer Season 8?

SA: It was a long time ago that we initially took it on, but I think it was another editor expressing a passion for the show. That was what I thought at the time, but lately I heard that it happened another way. That editor left the company, which led to me taking the comics on. We did a monthly comic for a number of years, and over that time I wound up working closely with Joss. When he told me the show was ending, I said I thought we should end the comics and restart them with a new directive from him. He agreed, and we started a long conversation about how we would do that, which went through a number of iterations. Ultimately, he took me by surprise. He sent me a script one night, no warning, said, 'We're doing 25 issues (or maybe it was 22), I'll write some of it, other guys from the show will write some of it, we'll do a crossover with Fray, and oh yeah, we need Angel back'. So it began ...

JKS: *From letter columns in the back of comic book issues, to interviews with media outlets both professional and amateur, you are very much engaged in maintaining a dialogue with* Buffy *fans. What inspires your dedication to this engagement, and what do you get out of it both personally and professionally? What do the fans teach you about the spirit of* Buffy?

Scott Allie, Dark Horse Comics

Fig.1: Buffy Summers leads
an army of Slayers in the
groundbreaking Buffy the
Vampire Slayer Season
8 comic book series - a
landmark in transmedia
storytelling.
©Dark Horse Comics

SA: The readers have a certain sense of ownership over this stuff, and talking with them is informative, among other things. I meet a lot of people I really like through it, who teach me a lot about what the characters mean to people. The folks at *Buffyfest* are good friends, Michelle over there is someone I call just to check in with sometimes, not even about Buffy. I really like a couple people on *Slayalive*, Wenxian and Emmie. Emmie's someone I don't always agree with, she certainly doesn't agree with me all the time, but I get a lot out of our exchanges. A woman named Maggie gives me great insight – again, we don't always agree, but there's a mutual level of respect that allows for a useful exchange of opinions that ultimately does more for me than it does for her. A lot of the Browncoats are among the best audience you could ever ask for, and there's a great population of them in Portland, so I actually run them into in the grocery store. Then you get a lot of weird stuff. One reader will e-mail me to tell me that some other reader I'm corresponding with from a particular site constantly posts negative things about me there. I don't know if it's true or not, can't take the time to check out the message board, but Jesus, guys, even these fictional characters have left high school behind. There's someone who never fails to tell me I'm doing a terrible job, have ruined her favourite characters, have hurt her personally, says really insulting things about how careless and thoughtless I am at my job […] and then she comes up to me at a show, says it's her birthday, and meeting me is the best birthday present she's ever had. And she's a grown woman, not a teenager.

JKS: *Do you find that most fans of the* Buffy *comics, canonical or other-*

wise, came from television fandom? Does it seem that they were comic book readers to begin with, or are they new to the medium? What are the demographics of readers of Season 8 *and* 9, *and* Angel & Faith? *Do you find that it's predominantly women, or is it balanced?*

SA: Yeah, certainly they largely come from TV. Think about how enormous even a 'cult' TV audience is. Millions, right? At the peak of it so far the comic has sold 150,000 copies, and the best-selling comic today might peak around 300,000. So the untapped former TV viewer audience is a far bigger number than the entire untapped comics market audience. I would say a majority of the Buffy comics audience, or at least the audience I hear from, are not regular comics readers, or were not. Lots of anecdotal evidence suggests that, including the feedback I get from retailers about the buying habits of *Buffy* readers. Also anecdotally, from letters and the like, I might surmise that Buffy readers tend to be women, but I suspect that it's fairly even and that the women are just writing in more. Certainly there are more female readers, proportionally, than on other comics.

JKS: *Response from fans to* Buffy the Vampire Slayer Season 8 *was mixed, though certainly, all new and experimental endeavours require evolution in order to strike the right balance. That said, how much did fan commentary influence the direction of* Buffy the Vampire Slayer Season 9?

SA: The general direction was influenced a lot by reader feedback, but mainly the part of reader feedback that we agreed with. There were things the readers said we didn't fully agree with, and that stuff probably hasn't changed. And I don't know that readers specifically said, possibly, 'We want smaller scale more personal stuff'. But we felt that doing that would address the basic gist of their concerns. We were playing. We were exploring a big field, and ultimately realized that not all of that field was right for us. We realized what these characters are best for, in this, or any, medium, which has led us to be careful to scale back the spectacle in order to give the characters more room to be themselves and explore their relationships, still in a colourful, action-adventure sort of way.

JKS: *What are some of the more meaningful responses you've received from Buffy fans? Most discouraging?*

SA: It runs pretty deep. Letters from gay kids or adults that thank us for what we do. The gratitude we got for addressing the abortion storyline. The most gratifying sort of response you can get is when someone writes in and explains exactly what they got out of a comic, and how it touched them, and what they got is exactly what you were trying to do. There are a lot of people who have gotten a lot of comfort from either the comics or the shows, who've felt the kind of pain maybe me or Joss or whomever felt at some point in our lives, and whatever catharsis the writers or artists got out of doing the comics, or the show, is reflected in the comfort that some part of the audience got. I don't get nearly as much of that out of other books. I don't get the sense of contributing on a social level from many of the other books I do. And it's gratifying.

JKS: *In 2011, Dark Horse co-hosted parties at regional comic book stores in celebration of Buffy's 30th birthday (30th in the television timeline) and the final issue of* Season 8. *Where did the idea originate for these celebrations? Do you know of other, perhaps unofficial, fan phenomena related specifically to the comics? Does Dark Horse have other tie-in celebrations planned for the future?*

SA: Probably that was Sierra's idea. I'm not sure. Maybe our events co-ordinator, Kari Yadro, who's a big *Buffy* fan. I can't remember where it came from. It might have been me who first had the idea to move *Buffy* from the first week of the month to the 19th, in order to hit her birthday. As I recall, Georges [Jeanty] was running behind, and the printers have a weird Christmas schedule, so it was looking like the book might be late. It was due out on the first Wednesday of January – all comics go on sale on Wednesdays, like DVDs and CDs go on sale on Tuesdays. Georges was looking like he might be late, and we noticed that her birthday was a Wednesday two weeks later, and it just came together. Where the parties came from, I don't know, and there's nothing like that planned right now. But I do know there were a bunch of other parties that we weren't directly involved in. Ours was at the library in downtown Portland, and we said a big video thank you to Joss that we e-mailed to him on the spot.

JKS: *Finally, the* Buffy *comics feel much like an act of fan phenomena in and of themselves, given that many of the creators and contributors hold the series close to their hearts. In your experience, how have you seen the fandom of the writers, producers, editors, illustrators and artists involved expressed in the production of Seasons 8 and 9, in spin-offs like* Angel & Faith, *and even in series like* Tales of the Slayers *and* Tales of the Vampires?

SA: Well, like me, many of the creators weren't fans until the work began. I'd never seen it, Georges had never seen it, even though I first contacted him years after the show ended. I don't think Christos Gage had seen much of it *[Ed. Note – Gage watched all seven seasons of BtVS and Angel the Series in preparation. – JKS]*. But the promise of a good job reached out to us, and we started watching, and we became genuine fans, and it's influenced the work we do on other projects. I know Chris's toolkit has expanded because of his work on the comics, and mine is practically defined by it now. We're fans of the material now, and we want to do justice to the characters as best we can, and I know for me, I want to take the things I like best about this kind of storytelling, Joss's way of writing, and explore it in the other projects I work on.

GO FURTHER

Websites

Dark Horse Comics, http://www.darkhorse.com/

Chapter
10

Unlimited Potentials:
Reflections of the Slayer

Arthur Smith and David Bushman

→ **Joss Whedon's signature creation was an act of subversion. What if, he wondered, a vulnerable young girl who takes a wrong turn down a dark alley and is set upon by predators […] turns around and kicks all kinds of ass? Thus was born Buffy the Vampire Slayer, a new archetype of female empowerment that has achieved iconic status on par with The Man with No Name and whose profound influence on popular culture shows no sign of abating.**

There had been tough female protagonists before Buffy – *The Terminator*'s (James Cameron, 1984) Sarah Connor and *Alien*'s (Ridley Scott, 1979) Ellen Ripley come to mind – but Buffy was something new and uniquely resonant. Buffy is emphatically a *girl*, slight and wide-eyed, and her strength derives not from the assumption of masculine attributes but from her compassion and self-acceptance. A sexual being neither victimized nor actualized through her sexuality, an emotional youth whose steely resolve did not preclude tenderness or whimsy, a relatable, fallible teenager terrified of her burgeoning responsibilities but determined to meet them, Buffy fully embraced flesh and blood girlhood and celebrated the strength inherent in that condition without compromise.

This chapter will explore the influence of Buffy as icon, on the subsequent creators and characters who have gone on to explore, refine, subvert and exalt this enduringly vital interpretation of girl power.

Kitty Pryde

If there's a bigger influence on Buffy than Kitty, I don't know what it was […]. She was an adolescent girl finding out she has great power and dealing with it.
– Joss Whedon, quoted in *New York Magazine* (2005)

Whedon's take on the comic book character Kitty Pryde stands as a fascinating example of the role of influence in pop culture; Kitty Pryde begets Buffy Summers, years later Whedon takes the reins of the X-Men, Buffy Summers informs Kitty Pryde, and the fans go wild: Whedon's stewardship of *The Astonishing X-Men* (2004) sold like fury, won an Eisner Award for best continuing series, and was crowned by industry bible *Wizard Magazine* as book of the year. Girl power, indeed.

Whedon has repeatedly cited the comic book character Kitty Pryde, member of the mutant superhero team the X-Men, as a primary inspiration for the creation of Buffy Summers. The parallels are obvious: Kitty, like Buffy, is an ordinary adolescent girl who, through an accident of birth, finds herself dealing with strange powers and frightening responsibilities that turn her heretofore mundane suburban existence upside down.

Like Buffy, Kitty was an essentially level-headed, responsible girl, interested in boys and dating but not defined by such concerns, and she similarly struggled to find the courage to face the terrifying circumstances in which the X-Men so often found themselves. Kitty's special mutant ability, the power to make her body insubstantial and 'phase' through solid objects like a ghost, was an evocative combination of vulnerability and strength; she possessed no special offensive capabilities beyond those of the average slightly built 14-year-old girl, but when employing her talent she theoretically could not be hurt. The converse of this dynamic is present in Buffy, a terrifically strong and resourceful combatant who nonetheless is only all too puncture-able flesh and blood. Kitty's youth, inexperience and lack of firepower often relegated her to a sort of jun-

Unlimited Potentials: Reflections of the Slayer
Arthur Smith and David Bushman

ior varsity status on the team and precluded her from taking a leadership role ... until, in a neat piece of pop culture symmetry, Joss Whedon took over writing duties on the *X-Men* after the conclusion of the *Buffy* series.

In his celebrated run on *The Astonishing X-Men*, Whedon unsurprisingly puts Kitty front and centre, the former ingenue now a mature and confident veteran of the hero game who functions as the tough yet compassionate heart of the team. Kitty gains a new foil in the person of Emma Frost, a hyper-sexualized (her wardrobe appears to consist entirely of white lingerie), haughty, statuesque psychic of questionable team loyalty who plays Cordelia to Kitty's Buffy. Their tetchy exchanges are a comic highlight of the run and help ground the action in relatable human interaction while providing Kitty with ample opportunity to deliver vintage Whedon snark. Kitty also demonstrates an impressive new adeptness in battle, exploiting her immaterial nature with a quick-and-dirty martial arts approach that echoes the improvisatory effectiveness of Buffy's vamp-dispatching style. Finally, in the emotionally fraught climax of Whedon's *X-Men* tenure, Kitty apparently sacrifices her life to protect the earth from an approaching alien projectile ... and dying to save the world is nothing if not a signature Buffy move.

Fig.1: Like Buffy, Rose Tyler (Billie Piper) inspires heroism in others
© BBC Wales

Rose Tyler

Russell T. Davies, the man responsible for rebooting the venerable British sci-fi series *Doctor Who* in 2005, specifically cites *Buffy* as an influence on both the show and on the character of Rose Tyler (Billie Piper), the Doctor's companion for the first two seasons (perhaps in acknowledgement, Rose earns a cameo in 'No Future for You', the third story arc of the *Buffy the Vampire Slayer Season 8* series of comic books). In a 2003 interview with *TV Times*, Davies said the new Doctor would

get a Buffy-style female sidekick [...] a modern action heroine. A screaming girly companion is unacceptable now [...] I don't mean in terms of women's rights – dramatically, we've got *Buffy the Vampire Slayer* now, so a screamingly girly companion would be laughed out of the room.

Rose, 19 years old when first encountered, is, like Buffy, petite, blonde and ostensibly unexceptional. Sharing a council flat in London with her widowed mum, Rose is a shop girl, toiling at a dead-end department-store job, having discontinued school in order to be with a chap who is no longer present in her life. Whereas Buffy's emergence as the Slayer is fated, Rose more or less stumbles into her role as world saviour: about to leave work one evening, she is dispatched back upstairs to make a drop-off, and is attacked by plastic mannequins (Autons) before the Doctor arrives to rescue her. The two then uncover – and ultimately foil – an alien plot to conquer the world. Late in the episode, Rose undergoes a transformative moment: with London under attack and the Doctor in peril, boyfriend Mickey urges her to 'just leave him […]. There's nothing you can do', but Rose ignores his advice, instead leaping into action as she liberates the Doctor from his captors. 'I've got no A-levels, no job, no future, but I tell you what I have got: Jericho Street Junior School Under-Sevens Gymnastics Team. I've got the bronze,' Rose tells Mickey, in a flash of Buffy-like banter (even the words 'the bronze', delivered at this crucial juncture in the emergence of Rose as action hero, can be interpreted as a wink at *Buffy*, evoking the Scooby Gang's favourite dive).

Over the course of two seasons, Rose steadily evolves into a stronger, more dynamic character; by 'Parting of the Ways', the Season 1 finale (Episode 13), she has been thoroughly transformed, from London shop-girl to Time Goddess: miserable at being stranded behind in contemporary London for her own safety by the Doctor, Rose, speaking of life aboard the TARDIS (the Doctor's travelling machine), tells Mickey and her mother:

It was a better life. And I – I don't mean all the travelling and seeing aliens and spaceships and things that don't matter. The Doctor showed me a better way of living your life. […] That you don't just give up. You don't just let things happen. You make a stand. You say no. You have the guts to do what's right when everyone else just turns away.

Rose not only finds a way back onto the TARDIS, but winds up saving the Doctor's life – again – and reviving Captain Jack Harness from the dead, granting him immortality in the process. In her 2010 book *Ink-Stained Amazons and Cinematic Warriors: Superwomen in Modern Mythology*, Jennifer K. Stuller writes of Buffy's 'compassionate heroism'; her actions (and the actions of other superwomen like her) 'not only save others, but also inspire them to find and perfect the heroic in themselves'. In *Doctor Who*, Rose functions in this same capacity, specifically with respect to the Doctor, infusing him with a level of humanity that had never existed in the character before, thus enhancing his own heroic stature.

Bo Dennis
Fans of *Lost Girl* (Michelle Lovretta, 2010), the Canadian supernatural crime drama, have been touting comparisons to *Buffy* via Twitter and other forums since the show premiered in its native country in 2010, two years before its US debut on Syfy. Like Buffy Summers, Bo Dennis (Anna Silk) is a superpowered 'other' – in this case, a succubus who feeds off the sexual energy of her partners, with the ability to steal their life force through a kiss, in addition to influencing their thought processes with her mere caress – seeking to come to terms with the implications of being, in Bo's own terminology, a 'freak'. Like Buffy, Bo is a character defined largely by her conscience and her independence, and she

Unlimited Potentials: Reflections of the Slayer
Arthur Smith and David Bushman

decides to leverage her power in the service of others; she and Kenzi, a post-goth pickpocket Bo rescues
from a date rapist in the premiere episode, open a detective agency (evoking another Whedonverse character as well, the vampire detective Angel).

Silk – a *Buffy* fan herself – has eagerly embraced
Bo's similarities to the Slayer in interviews, empha-
sizing their very human qualities, particularly their
doubts and insecurities about who they are, despite their supernatural talents: '[Buffy]
was kind of like your every girl; she just happened to be a vampire slayer, and that's what
I liked about Bo when I first read the script', she told the Canadian Press. Silk added that
'I like how strong [Bo] can be, but I love how scared she is'.

Lost Girl creator Michelle Lovretta also embraces the comparisons to Buffy, saying
that Bo shares the slayer's 'sense of both loss and wonder when she realizes she's not the
"normal girl" she thought she was'. Still, Bo isn't nearly as angst-ridden as Buffy. While
shows like *Buffy*, *Dark Angel* (James Cameron and Charles H. Eglee, 2000-02) and *Heroes* (Tim Kring, 2006-10) leveraged the teen-superhero genre to delve metaphorically
into the traumas of adolescence, *Lost Girl* is – in the words of Lovretta, 'a goofy-ass
show, and I say that with love. That's one of the things about it that I think is charming – it
has fun with itself'. Nowhere is this variance more pronounced than in Bo's passionate,
guilt-free indulgence in sex, which accompanies her self-awareness as a succubus (a
profound reorientation for a woman who earlier had lamented that her love 'carries a
death sentence'): *Lost Girl*, wrote Alyssa Rosenberg in 2012, 'represents, in television
terms, a generation of forward progress from *Buffy* when it comes to sex. Sex is literally
life-giving to Bo, rather than conflicted in the many ways it is in *Buffy*'.

Fig.2: Hanna (Saoirse Ronan), like Buffy, subverts a female pop culture stereotype © 2011 Focus Features, Holleran Company, Sechzehnte Babelsberg Film

Hanna
The release of a number of theatrical films with assertive, powerful adolescent female
characters from 2009–11, including *Sucker Punch* (Zack Snyder, 2011), *Kick-Ass* (Matthew Vaughn, 2010) and *Hanna* (Joe Wright, 2011), led to a wave of newspaper, magazine
and Internet articles identifying a new breed of superwoman – or, more accurately –
supergirl (the 'petite tough girl', one wag dubbed it). In the 17 April 2011 edition of the
Detroit News, Tom Long called this paradigm the new 'Bad Girl': 'She's young. She's hot.
She'll slit your throat without giving it a second thought'. Tom Long dubbed these new
superheroines 'Buffy's children', arguing that many of today's young writers, directors
and producers grew up watching *Buffy*, and that 'the image of a sexually attractive-ac-
tive young woman bloodying baddies has been drilled into the common consciousness
through a number of post-*Buffy* TV shows over the years'.

In *Hanna*, Saoirse Ronan stars as the titular character, a 16-year-old girl (the same
age as Buffy when *BtVS* premiered) who, as the film opens, is being raised in the isolated

tundra of northern Finland by a man named Erik, whom she believes to be her father. When first seen, Hanna is hunting a deer, which she proceeds to kill, and eviscerate with her bare hands. We soon discover that Erik is training Hanna to become an assassin, with the target being Marissa Wiegler, a sinister CIA agent who years earlier had killed Hanna's mother and attempted to kill Erik and Hanna as well. It is eventually revealed that Erik is not Hanna's father, but rather an erstwhile government operative who recruited pregnant women, including Hanna's mother, from abortion clinics to participate in a CIA-run program to create super-soldiers through DNA-altering experiments intended to bolster strength and diminish human capacity for pity and fear. The program succeeded like gangbusters; Hanna is replete with gorgeously designed sequences of the lethal teenager dispatching her many pursuers with cold, steely elegance ... she kills without hesitation, and hardly seems to break a sweat.

Just as Joss Whedon conceived of *Buffy* as a subversion of the pretty blonde horror-movie victim, *Hanna* director Joe Wright has been very outspoken in his intention to present Ronan's character as a counterpoint to the highly sexualized action hero, particularly of the young-girl variety. As Tom Huddleston reported on 5 May 2011 in *Time Out*, Wright said, in response to the question of whether *Hanna* is a feminist movie: 'I specifically wanted to avoid "sexing up" Hanna. I didn't want her in a fucking mini-skirt or crop top. I'm very alarmed by the continued sexual objectification of young women'. Wright rather famously made the same point at a Wondercon panel, where he specifically cited the film *Sucker Punch* as a culprit.

Baby Doll

Sucker Punch, Zach Snyder's lurid 2011 fantasia/satire of fanboy tropes, presents one of the most problematic of Buffy's descendants, the much abused yet preternaturally lethal Baby Doll. The uneasiness begins with the character's name, a double whammy of infantilized sexuality that is compounded by actress Emily Browning's fetishistic 'schoolgirl fantasy' appearance, all ponytails, huge blank eyes and artfully exposed flesh. The plot of *Sucker Punch* is an utterly confounding stew of gothic clichés and sick pornographic fantasies; whether the difficulty in following the story is a deliberate narrative strategy or merely the result of the film-maker's incompetence is perhaps open for discussion, but the premise is something like this: a young woman is committed to a mental institution by her widowed stepfather after she witnesses him killing her sister in the midst of an implied sexual assault. For reasons that remain unclear, our heroine is scheduled for a lobotomy in five days' time, effectively shutting her up forever. While ensconced in the asylum, Baby Doll retreats into a fantasy world (or does she?) in which the hospital becomes a brothel featuring her and her impossibly attractive fellow inmates as prostitutes/exotic dancers. Why this would be the escapist scenario chosen by our heroine is never addressed, but the movie goes yet another layer deeper (calling to mind some unholy union of *Inception* [Christopher Nolan, 2010] and a late-night softcore cable mov-

Unlimited Potentials: Reflections of the Slayer
Arthur Smith and David Bushman

ie), in which Baby Doll's dance routines morph into video game-like battle scenarios in which the intrepid inmates/prostitutes/dancers take out legions of out-sized foes including giant steampunk samurai warriors, zombie WWI soldiers, and, what the hell, a dragon.

None of it makes a lick of sense. There is some folderol about an escape attempt being carried out along the various metaphorical (Or literal? Who knows?) parallel realities, but the film is clearly primarily concerned with delivering spectacular visuals, creepy titillation and cathartic violence. Snyder claimed that his film was meant as a satirical critique of the ugly, voyeuristic aspects of sci-fi fandom, his aim presumably to deconstruct the Buffy-derived trope of the nubile ass-kicker. This is a potentially rich subject – we can all agree that there is much to value in the post-Buffy archetype of the strong girl warrior, but what are the less savoury elements of this character type's appeal? Snyder's film, though, is woefully inadequate to the task, oppressively over-designed and narratively undernourished, and the constant threat and implication of rape are so heavy-handed that they preclude any nuanced apprehension of the film's ostensible subject. *Sucker Punch* is an uncommonly depressing, claustrophobic experience, and Baby Doll is Buffy without agency, depth or resonance ... Buffy reduced to a sex toy who kills, an avatar in a prurient video game, a repository of the basest male fantasies and creatively exhausted fantasy tropes. Snyder might say that's exactly the point, but absent any degree of theoretical rigour or artistic intelligence, *Sucker Punch* does no more than live up to its name.

Fig.3: Hit-Girl (Chloe Moretz) took the notion of girl power to its psychopathic extreme © 2010; Marv Films, Plan B Entertainment, Universal Pictures, Lionsgate Films

Hit Girl

If Baby Doll represents a troubling interpretation of the Buffy archetype, the character of Hit Girl, from the comic book (Mark Millar and John Romita Jr., 2008-10) and film *Kick-Ass*, is downright apocalyptic. An adorable pre-pubescent who gleefully slashes her way through platoons of malefactors, Hit Girl is the nihilistic endpoint of the post-Buffy warrior girl character. Her extreme youth and ostensible attendant innocence are played for sick joke as she expertly wields a variety of edged weapons to inflict maximum trauma, all the while expressing the irrepressible joy of a kid enjoying the best theme park ride *ever*.

Her vigilante father, Big Daddy, a psychopathic ex-cop with a more-than-passing resemblance to Batman, is outfitted with an arsenal and wages a war on crime aided by his adorable daughter, whom he has trained as a vicious death-dealer in a grotesque parody of filial devotion. This relationship is superficially identical to the dynamic between the title character and her paternal protector in *Hanna*, but where that film portrayed Eric Bana's Spartan parenting routine as gravely tender and tragically necessary, *Kick-Ass* presents its father/daughter relationship as a grotesque joke: one of the movie's biggest comedic moments involves Big Daddy unexpectedly shooting his tiny daughter repeatedly in the chest (she is wearing Kevlar under her cute tween outfit) before showering her with cloying encouragement, as if she just scored a tricky goal in a soccer game. *Buffy* often dealt with the theme of the damage done by absent fathers; *Kick-Ass* suggests that a present and enthusiastically involved dad may be much worse.

 Kick-Ass is rife with scenes of Hit Girl brutally killing her opponents, and a deeply disturbing sequence in which she is subdued and brutalized by the head of the mob family, but, perhaps predictably, it was a piece of dialogue that elicited the greatest controversy. Hit Girl, taunting a group of thugs before graphically separating them from their limbs, contemptuously calls them 'cunts'. Apparently the image of a small girl racking up bloody body counts is one thing, but having her swear is a bridge too far. The complicated response Hit Girl evoked in *Kick-Ass*'s audience – shocked amusement, the thrill of a novel new form of ultra-violence, hand-wringing over the debasement of a child – suggests that the post-Buffy ass-kicker contains reserves of thematic richness and narrative surprise that have merely been tapped, and that while Hanna, Baby Doll, Hit Girl and the rest all resemble their spiritual big sister Buffy in various ways, creators will continue to ring endless variations on this unusually potent new archetype. One of the most popular Halloween costumes for young girls in 2010 was Hit Girl's stylish, Manga-influenced ensemble. Whether this is encouraging or disturbing is open for debate.

Katniss Everdeen

The Buffy descendant that has had the most significant impact on popular culture is unquestionably Katniss Everdeen, the conflicted heroine of Suzanne Collins's phenomenally popular *Hunger Games* trilogy (2008-10); as of this writing, there are 26 million copies of the books in print, and the feature film adaptation was a runaway success, earning more than 150 million dollars in the first weekend of its release. Katniss, like Buffy, is a young teenaged girl boasting superior physical skills compelled to engage in deadly combat against seemingly insurmountable odds. Katniss's world is a post-war dystopia in which poverty-stricken agricultural and manufacturing 'Districts' support a decadent 'Capitol', which annually requires a sampling of the Districts' children to fight to the death in a baroque sporting event broadcast for the entertainment of the pampered Capitol residents and the intimidation of the District dwellers, who had previously rebelled and brought about some great unexplained catastrophe. At the beginning of the story, Katniss is a wary, withdrawn girl who has developed superlative hunting abilities – she is a crack-shot archer – to provide forbidden game for

Fig.3: Katniss Everdeen (Jennifer Lawrence) faces impossible responsibilities with grim determination, much like our favorite slayer © 2012; Lionsgate, Color Force

Unlimited Potentials: Reflections of the Slayer
Arthur Smith and David Bushman

her starving family. Katniss's existence, like Buffy's, is ruled by a grim sense of responsibility and duty, and, without a support system like Buffy's Scooby Gang, Katniss grows up emotionally distant, suspicious and prematurely cynical, vulnerable only in her concern for and devotion to her frail younger sister, Prim.

Katniss's 'hero's journey' commences when Prim is selected for inclusion in the Games and our heroine volunteers to compete in her stead. Throughout the bloody trials that follow, Katniss moves from private concerns – her survival and the welfare of her family – to a reluctant sort of compassion, befriending a younger and more vulnerable contestant, Prue, to ultimately developing a political consciousness beyond the Games. Katniss acquires a sort of Scooby Gang along the way, including Cinna, a savvy stylist whose ministrations allow the initially quasi-feral poor girl from the poorest district to capture the public's attention, and Haymitch, a dissolute but wily former winner of the Games who serves as Katniss's mentor and surrogate father figure and who, like Buffy's Giles, counsels his charge in the deadly realities of her unwanted occupation. Drawing strength and courage from her new friends, Katniss is able to fully exploit her inherent toughness and magnetism to not only triumph in the draconian Games, but to galvanize the oppressed District citizens and lead a full-scale rebellion against the corrupt Capitol, evolving into a Messianic figure, the erstwhile huntress now a symbol of hope.

Katnisws follows Buffy's path from frightened neophyte, invested with great potential but untested, to competent combatant, deadly but compassionate, to fully self-actualized leader and inspiration, a source of strength for the forces of good. An old story, and as deeply satisfying as ever, as evidenced by The Hunger Games's status as a legitimate cultural phenomenon.

Conclusion
Buffy the Vampire Slayer has taken her place as an archetype of female empowerment that has achieved iconic status and whose profound influence on popular culture shows no sign of abating. Post-Whedon creators have reckoned with this endlessly compelling, frequently empowering, occasionally troubling new vision of feminist power and self-determination to uniformly edifying results; even the less successful iterations have much to teach us about how we value or fear the strength of women. Whedon's great creation continues to inform every new ass-kicking girl to grace the page or tube or screen. It is to his credit, and our benefit, that Buffy did it first with such grace, style, humour and heart. ●

GO FURTHER

Books

Ink-Stained Amazons and Cinematic Warriors: Superwomen in Modern Mythology

Jennifer K. Stuller
(London and New York: I.B. Tauris & Co Ltd, 2010)

Back to the Vortex: The Unofficial and Unauthorized Guide to 'Doctor Who 2005'
J Shaun Lyon
(England: Telos Publishing Ltd., 2005)

Extracts/Essays/Articles

'"Lost Girl" Isn't "Buffy the Vampire Slayer" – And That's Okay'
Alyssa Rosenberg
ThinkProgress. 3 April 2012, http://thinkprogress.org/alyssa/2012/04/03/457055/lost-girl-isnt-buffy-the-vampire-slayerand-thats-okay/?mobile=nc.

'In the writer's room with not-so-Lost Girl Michelle Lovretta'
Katie Bailey
PlayBack. 13 January 2012, http://playbackonline.ca/2012/01/13/in-the-writers-room-with-not-so-lost-girl-michelle-lovretta/.

'"Lost Girl" star Anna Silk drops inhibitions to play seductive succubus Bo'
Victoria Ahearn
Western Wheel. 1 September 2011.

'Atonement' director kicks ass; He's known for more literary fare, but director Joe Wright has made an action flick with young Saoirse Ronan. Tom Huddleston asks him why
Tom Huddleston
Time Out. 5 May 2011. Pg. 78.

'Young, violent femmes attack the big screen'
Tom Long
Detroit News. 7 April 2011. Pg. M8.

'Nine Questions with Lost Girl Creator and Writer Michelle Lovretta'
Alex "drsquid' Davies
RGB Filter. 30 September 2010, http://www.rgbfilter.com/?p=10538.

'Whedon, Ink'
Gavin Edwards
New York Magazine. 21 May 2005, http://nymag.com/nymetro/arts/9218/

Contributor Details

EDITOR

Jennifer K. Stuller is a professional writer, critic, scholar, pop culture historian, public speaker, and the author of *Ink-Stained Amazons and Cinematic Warriors: Superwomen in Modern Mythology* (I.B. Tauris, 2010). As a feminist and a historian, her particular interests focus on what popular culture reveals about social mores, particularly regarding gender, race, sexuality, ability, religion and class, in a given time or place. A regular contributor to national publications and organizations, including Bitch Media, Ms Stuller has been invited to speak at conferences in the United States and internationally, and provided expert opinion and interviews for radio, newspapers and documentaries including, *Wonder Women! The Untold Story of American Superheroines* (Kristy Guevara-Flanagan, 2012), for which she also served as a consultant. She is a Charter Associate member of the Whedon Studies Association, and a co-founder of, and the programming director for, GeekGirlCon – an organization dedicated to the recognition, encouragement and support of women's accomplishments, interests and contributions to Geek Culture including pop culture industries and STEM professions. She lives in Seattle with her husband, and their two Maltese, Giles and Wesley, and can be found at www.ink-stainedamazon.com.

CONTRIBUTORS

Kristen Julia Anderson is a fan of fantasy and sci-fi works such as *Star Wars*, *Lord of the Rings* and of course, *Buffy the Vampire Slayer*, which has inspired her both professionally and personally. She has published her creative works online; this publication marks her first non-fiction and book contribution. Throughout her experiences with higher education, be they as a student or instructor, *Buffy* has been a constant companion. Anderson's thesis analysed the rhetoric of a *Buffy* online fanfiction community, and she presented on *Buffy* at the 2012 NEPCA conference. Anderson feels lucky to marry her fan interests with her academic and career ones. A graduate of Montclair State University's English MA writing studies program, she currently works as an adjunct professor and library assistant. Her syllabi, when possible, include units and assignments about *Buffy* and other Whedon creations, often focusing on the representations of gender, family and society.

David Bushman is a television curator at The Paley Center for Media in New York, where he has organized a number of screening series over the past twenty years, including retrospective looks at presidential-campaign advertising, the programming of the Canadian Broadcasting Corporation, and the evolution of the stand-up comedian on television. He previously was programming director at the cable channel TV Land, where he fought valiantly but futilely to bring *The Avengers* and *The Defenders* back to television, and a television editor at *Daily Variety* and *Variety*, and has taught and lectured on media at colleges and other institutions. His particular area of expertise is television noir, and he is currently at work on a book on the subject.

David Boarder Giles is a doctoral candidate in sociocultural anthropology at the University of Washington, Seattle. His research and teaching deals with the ethnography of global cities, waste, homelessness and grassroots social movements. He has also taught courses on the anthropology of popular culture and mass media at the University of Washington. He is originally from Melbourne, Australia, and has a long-standing love of science fiction and fantasy – especially those stories in which badass women get to save the day.

Tanya R. Cochran, Ph.D. – an associate professor of English at Union College in Lincoln, NE, Cochran teaches first-year writing and the history/theory of rhetoric, directs the College Writing Program and steers the Studio for Writing and Speaking. She is a founding board member of the Whedon Studies Association as well as its current president (2012–14) and serves on the editorial boards of *Slayage: The Journal of the Whedon Studies Association* and its undergraduate equivalent *Watcher Junior*. Among others, her publications include chapters in *Televising Queer Women* (Palgrave, 2008) and *Siths, Slayers, Stargates + Cyborgs: Modern Mythology in the New Millennium* (Peter Lang, 2008). With Rhonda V. Wilcox, Cochran edited the anthology *Investigating Firefly and Serenity: Science Fiction on the Frontier* (I.B. Tauris, 2008). Her most recent work appears in the journal *Transformative Works and Cultures*. Forthcoming is *A Joss Whedon Reader* (Syracuse University Press), a collection edited with David Lavery, Cynthea Masson and Wilcox.

Nikki Faith Fuller earned her BA in Psychology and MA in English and currently teaches English Composition and literature courses in sunny California. She wrote her Master's thesis on *Buffy the Vampire Slayer*, examining it from the perspective of Joseph Campbell's hero's journey. She is currently working on her Ph.D. in the Mythological Studies with an emphasis in Depth Psychology. She can be found at mythgirl.org and twitter.com/myth_girl.

Lorna Jowett is Reader in Television Studies at the University of Northampton, UK. She is the author of *Sex and the Slayer: A Gender Studies Primer for the Buffy Fan* (Wesleyan University Press, 2005) and co-author with Stacey Abbott of *TV Horror: Investigating the Dark Side of the Small Screen* (I.B. Tauris, 2012). She has published many articles on gender and genre in television, film and popular culture, and is on the editorial board of *Slayage: The Journal of the Whedon Studies Association*.

Mary Kirby-Diaz is a professor of sociology at Farmingdale State College – SUNY. Her areas of expertise are fandom studies, mass media and popular culture (movies, music and fashion), urban sociology and marriage. Her professional work focuses on community, marginalization, loneliness and love. Much as Mary loved both *Buffy* ('Vampire Slayer extraordinaire') and *Angel*, she discovered that she was more interested in the fans and the fandom. That interest created 'The Fandom Project', a long-term, multi-method study of *BtVS* and *AtS*'s online fandoms, which culminated in several publications, including *Buffy and Angel Conquer the Internet* (McFarland, 2009).

Liz Medendorp is a graduate student at the University of Massachusetts, Amherst pursuing a Master's degree in Translation Studies. Her research focus is on popular culture and new media studies and she has participated in several academic conferences as a scholar of the musical mash-up phenomenon and its ties to participatory culture, the moral structure of *Buffy the Vampire Slayer*, and the impact of video games on society. She received her BA degree with high honours from the University of Michigan in French Language and Literature, and has worked in particular on the translation of French-language comics and graphic novels into English. In her thesis she plans to explore concepts of intersemiotic translation within the works of Joss Whedon, in particular *Buffy the Vampire Slayer* and *Firefly*.

Anthony R. Mills is an independent scholar who focuses on the intersections between pop culture media and fandom, geek culture, religion, philosophy and cognitive science. He received a Ph.D. in Theology and Culture from Fuller Theological Seminary in Pasadena, California where he wrote a dissertation on American mythology, Marvel Comics and theological anthropology. He is co-editor of an anthology of essays entitled *Joss Whedon and Religion* (McFarland, forthcoming), blogs at cardinaltony.blogspot.com, and has a podcast with friends at fourgeeksandamicrophone.podbean.com.

Amy Peloff is Assistant Director of the Comparative History of Ideas Program and Affiliate Assistant Professor of Gender, Women and Sexuality Studies at the University of Washington. Her work examines the role that popular culture has played in disseminating feminist ideas beyond the organizations and activists that identified as feminist in the United States, particularly during the second wave of feminism. A voracious consumer of female detective stories, sci-fi and fantasy television series, and Hollywood gossip, she continually studies the ways in which ideas about identities are created, presented, and shared through media and popular culture.

Arthur Smith has been with the Paley Center for Media's curatorial department for fifteen years, where he has written extensively about media and curated screening series celebrating the histories of pop music, sketch comedy and the horror genre on television, among many others. He is also a contributor to *Kirkus Reviews*, specializing on books related to the entertainment industry, and has worked as an advertising copywriter and freelance magazine contributor. His band is called Zombies of the Stratosphere, but he's not a particular fan of zombies, or of the stratosphere, for that matter.

Image Credits

From Buffy the Vampire Slayer
Chapter 1:   Fig. 1 p.13
             Fig. 4 p.15
Chapter 4:   Fig. 1 p.65
             Fig. 4 p.70
Chapter 5:   Figs. 1-3 pages 75, 76 & 78
Chapter 6:   Fig. 1 p.92
Chapter 7:   Fig. 1 p.104
             Fig. 2 p.109 © 20th Century Fox Television

Additional Images
Introduction: Fig. 1 p.6 © Inti St. Clair
Chapter 1:   Fig. 2 p.14 © Dark Horse Comics
             Fig. 3 p.15 © Warner Brothers
             Fig. 5 p.16 © Inti St. Clair
Fan Appreciation 1: Fig. 1 p.52 © Nikki Stafford
Chapter 4:   Fig. 2 p.66 ©AP/Damian Dovarganes
             Fig. 3 p.67 © Thomas Coleman and Michael Rosenblatt Productions
Fan Appreciation 2: Fig. 1 p.84 © Richard Gess
Chapter 6:   Fig. 2 p.93 ©HBO and ©Your Face Goes Here Entertainment
Chapter 8:   Fig. 1 p.116 ©Joey Spiotto
             Fig. 2 p.117 ©Megan-Jayne McFall
             Fig. 3 ©Agnes Barton-Sabo
Fan Appreciation 3: Fig. 1 p.120 ©Clinton McClung
             Figs. 2-3 p.126 ©Guy Eats Octopus
Fan Appreciation 4: Fig. 1 p.144 ©Jessie Christiansen
             Fig. 2 p.146 ©Dark Horse Comics
Chapter 10: Fig. 1 p.152 ©BBC
             Fig. 2 p.154 ©Focus Features
             Fig. 3 p.156 ©Marv Films, Plan B Entertainment,
             Universal Pictures, Lionsgate Films;
             Fig. 4 p.157 ©Lionsgate, Color Force